INSINCERELY YOURS

INSINCERELY YOURS
LETTERS FROM A PRANKSTER

By BERNARD RADFAR

Rare Bird Books
Los Angeles | New York

This is A Rare Bird Book

Copyright © 2012 by Bernard Radfar

Distributed in the U.S. by Publishers Group West

Printed in the United States of America.

For information and inquiries, address Rare Bird Books, 453 South Spring Street, Suite 531, Los Angeles, CA 90013.

Design by Erika Terriquez
Set in Goudy Old Style

Cataloging-in-Publication Data for this book is available from the Library of Congress.

ISBN-13: 978-0-9839255-1-4

10 9 8 7 6 5 4 3 2 1

This book is dedicated to the love and example of
Nazee, Yona, Hannah, and Elias.

CONTENTS

PREFACE

On September 5, 2010, I, Bernard Radfar, conceived Mark Black. He'd been lurking inside for years, an eccentric prankster threatening to carve out a place in my life. It wasn't clear at first whether he would be accepted by anyone outside my skull. But the world beckoned him, and there was no holding him back.

As a writer of novels and screenplays, I generally lock out reality, so that I can invent my own. I hide from people to create people. My admiration for those who confront people and bend lives toward the unreal borders on worship. Sacha Baron Cohen, the brash comedic phenom, is only the latest in a brave army of surrealist imps whose ranks reach back through Andy Kaufman, Fernando Pessoa, Marcel Duchamp, and Salvador Dalí.

My closets are full of correspondences with people from all walks of life. When we write letters (or communicate by any techno-device, or even face to face), the setup forces the receiver to reply. The answer is usually contained in the question. The worker at a fast food drive-thru isn't really asking how you're doing. Yet only the shackles of etiquette keep you from describing in goose-pimpling detail your argument with your lover. That's what Mark Black would do.

It was my job, as Mark Black, to exploit the power of a sender's message, testing whether—and how—people would reply to his kooky requests.

They responded in every manner imaginable. One cantankerous artist threatened to call the police. But many ignored the odd aspects of the communication, swept away by promises of financial reward. If I insult or confuse you, but you sense that you can make a buck off me, you may not mind. Avarice often trumps dignity.

Mark Black intends no malice, usually. Satire possesses, at its heart, a moral cry for reality—or at least for the human experience of it—to be other than it is. I'd love to live in a world where people think more and believe less. But we are all involved every day in the grand scheme of the human comedy. Some invest more deeply in the farce than others. I am probably one of those. It is in my own relationship to myself that I most exquisitely encounter the absurdity of existence.

Thank you to all those who've stood beside me on this long journey as author—and as Mark Black. You know who you are. In particular, Claire Gerus, who took the gamble to represent my writing, and does so with full gusto and grace, as well as Tyson Cornell, who has been as generous a friend and publisher as I could dream up. Had it not been for you, Mark Black would still be trapped inside. The world would be infinitely less meaningful without you.

I now hand the mic to Mark Black.

Bernard Radfar
Latitude: 35.664895
Longitude: 139.766915

We are what we pretend to be, so we must be careful about what we pretend to be.
—KURT VONNEGUT

At any street corner the feeling of absurdity can strike any man in the face.
—ALBERT CAMUS

CHAPTER ONE
MARK'S TRAVEL NEEDS

Dear Greyhound Bus Lines,
My lover and I live part of the year in a small city in Germany called
Konigsberg, and we want to come to the USA to travel across your
country by bus. Our friends and parents tell us it is wonderful. I am
curious about your driving methods, particularly on the West Coast,
near Oregon. Is it expected that your drivers will use cruise control?

I like to read medieval metaphysical books when I travel, and, in
general, I've found that traveling by cruise control is far superior to
being subjected to a driver's foot control, accelerating and decelerating.

Are your drivers expected to use cruise control whenever possible?
You wouldn't believe it, but I was in northern Ghana this year, and
the bus driver refused to use the cruise control. If I ever see him again
I will give him a piece of my mind. Now I always have to ask before I
make final scheduling decisions about my travel.

Please let me know soon so I can begin planning our adventure.
My lover is so excited.
Good day,
Mark Black

Dear Mr. Black:

Thank you for your e-mail and interest in traveling with Greyhound Lines.

Regarding your question, in this particular case, our Bus Drivers are trained to and advised to conduct the vehicles and transport the passengers under their care with the outmost precaution and maximum consideration to comfort and safety, always taking every precaution, to the maximal capacity and its farthest extent, no matter how minimum the risk to ensure you'll have a great trip with us.

The Cruise Control system, however, is just one tool that can be applied or not to the route and the area of travel according to their judgment and their rigorous training and experience.

However, for a more direct answer on their capabilities and the parameters of driving on this area, as the geography of a given area and topography condition the use of these systems, you may need to contact our Customer Service department, from 7:00 a.m. to 7:00 p.m. Central Time, U.S. Monday to Friday at their number to revise their information on the specific procedures and driving parameters as well as mechanical information.

If you have any further questions, please feel free to contact us again. Please include this e-mail with your response.

Sincerely,

Joseph K.

Web Support Team

Dear Government of Santa Monica,

It is my wish to celebrate the solstice this year with my new lover from Saudi Arabia, who will be meeting me in your city. I have been after her for over twenty-two years, ever since I met her in a canoe off the Alaskan coast. We were both looking for sockeye salmon.

I'm writing you today because I would like to inquire about the possibility of acquiring a license for a weekend permit to travel through Santa Monica and park somewhere near one of the finer hotels on the beach, an elephant. I promised her that we would travel by elephant. The two of us pose no danger or risk to the elephant because, combined, we are rather small and light, 280 lbs. total. Each is 140 lbs.

I would be bringing the elephant from New Mexico by Toyota truck.

I look forward to hearing from you soon.

Mark Black

Konigsberg, Germany

Mr. Black,

Greeting from Santa Monica!

I appreciate your admiration and affection for the one you love, but the City of Santa Monica will be unable to grant your request. The beachfront in the City of Santa Monica actually is a California State Beach and regulated by Santa Monica Municipal Codes as well as state law. The California Code of Regulations (CCR) title 17, section 7985.1, states "No person shall bring onto or allow any animal, except guide dogs used by the blind, to remain on any beach which has been designated a public swimming beach by the state, or any city, county, or city and county and where lifeguards are provided, except that horses may be ridden on designated equestrian trails and areas."

Good luck to you in the future.

Sergeant Joshua Mueller
Animal Control Unit
Santa Monica Police Department

D<small>ear</small> Mr. Mueller,

If I choose to ride the elephant would you ticket me, jail me, and/or take the elephant away?

Thank you for writing, truly.

Mark Black

M_{r.} Black,

I must admit that I am astonished that you would ask such a question after you have been advised of the rules and regulations. You may not bring an elephant to Santa Monica or ride it on the beach. Failure to comply may result in a citation, arrest, and the animal confiscated. Please reconsider your decisions and plans. Again, if you have any further question, please feel free to call or e-mail.

Sergeant Joshua Mueller

Dear India Concierge International,
I am thinking of coming to India next month with three women.
One lover is very tall and from Latvia. Another lover is a passionate,
but very short woman from Saudi Arabia, and the third is my sister
from Philadelphia. Coincidentally, each of us is 140 lbs. Anyhow, we
560 pounds are thinking of coming to India and traveling around the
country in my Latvian girlfriend's bulletproof Aston Martin vehicle. I
have a few questions:

1. Will we be safe in places like Kashmir and Uttar Pradesh?
2. Can you guarantee that we will not get sick from the food in India?
3. If I do not want to smell curry, will it be impossible to travel?
4. Would it be possible to travel with a portable bidet? If not, can you
recommend places to stay along the way that offer sanitary colonics?

I would like the concierge to meet us at each end of our journey.
I don't want to talk to people in the country and would like the
concierge to handle all our daily requirements besides driving. I will
not be eating any Indian cuisine while there, so arrangements must
be made. Everything must be VIP, and everything must be organized
as if it were Switzerland. I will pay fully, plus baksheesh, if this is all
executed with mastery.
Thank you,
Mark Black
Konigsberg, Germany

Dear Mr. Mark,

Greetings for the day from India. Thank you very much for your mail regarding travel to India on private tour. We noted your personal detail also. As per your mail you don't need transportation from our end as you are bringing with you one of the most beautiful cars to India. We would not recommend you to visit Kashmir due to security reason and of course you can visit other parts of India such as Historical Rajasthan, Uttar Pradesh and most beautiful state—Kerala.

As we knew that you have one month time to visit India, we noted but we want to know the category of hotels you need to stay? Meal plan? And flight—eco or business class if required.

Of course food are 100% safe if you go for high category of hotels, we will manage you hotel accommodation and for the activities you can consult with Concierge for daily activities. Kindly revert with the dates and other detail we need as per our mail above. As soon as we receive the detail from you (names etc.) we can go ahead for reservations and arrangements.

Note: Please advice us what is your travel plan during the one month which you have planned out.

Thanks & Regards,

Aniruddha for India Concierge International

Dear Jumeirah Group and Burj Hotel,
I am thinking of inviting my friends to stay at the Seven Star Burj
Hotel in November, on our way back from Saudi Arabia. We would
like to stay in the Royal Suite, though we are not royalty, if that is
your largest one, and wonder what is the maximum number of people
allowed? That is the number of people I will bring. We are rather small
in height and weight so that is not a consideration when you mention
the numbers. I would keep my staff on a lower level, if you don't mind.
My issue is whether your hotel has falafel and if the falafel are of high
quality. My close friends are particular connoisseurs of falafels and
would like to know the approximate diameter of your falafel. If they
are large or oily or filled with greens, Egyptian style, they ask if you
could make them Levantine. These friends are highly discerning, and
I've made the mistake before with them when we went to Beirut on
a similar vacation. It ruined the trip when the falafel were discovered
to be problematic. I couldn't tell the difference, but they forced us to
leave the hotel. Because your hotel is as well-reputed as it is I figured
you were the people to contact this time.
I look forward to hearing from you,
Mark Black
Montecito, California

D_{ear} Mark,

Thank you for your e-mail. We have noted your below e-mail, kindly advise us the exact arrival & departure date in order send you the rates and availability. The Royal Suites, of which there are two (2), spread over the 25th floor, are 780 square meters in area. Palatial surroundings reach unsurpassed peaks of luxury, including a private elevator, private cinema, rotating beds, Majlis (Arabic meeting room), and even dressing rooms larger than the average hotel bedroom. This suite can accommodate four adults and two children below 12 years of age or five adults only.

We have noted your food preferences, and therefore I have attached the recipe of the falafel which was created by our Executive Oriental Chef, Mohammed Eddine. Please be advised that we can prepare falafel in any sizes (mini, cocktail, etc.) and is really up to our guest preferences.

Should you require any further clarifications and assistance, please do not hesitate to contact us.

Kind Regards,

Omar Bargouthi, Suite Reservations

Burj Al Arab Hotel

Dear Italian Bicycle Adventures,
I am considering reserving a bike trip with a woman whom I have an obsession for. She is from Saudi Arabia, and I have to do whatever I can to woo her. Nothing works. I took her to Spain, and in the middle of an El Bulli dessert she started crying and screaming. She nearly threw her shoe at me. I was humiliated, and I paid the bill with cash and ran out of there. I can never look Ferran Adrian in the face again.

She has a tendency to do this when I make my best gestures towards her.

That brings me to your bike tour. I would like to know if we are on a tandem bike or if we have separate bikes. I would like to know what you'll do to keep us from getting lost, because she has been known to intentionally get me lost. I have fears of abandonment, more or less. I would like to know your refund policy, in case of one of her tantrums. I shall try to schedule the trip so that her hormones are in order, but I can't guarantee her full cooperation on the tour. I wouldn't feel right letting her spoil it for the others. I have even considered bringing along her psychotherapist, who would vacation in a car while we bike Italy.

It is my dream to do so. I hope you can help me fulfill this wish.
Sincerely,
Mark Black
Montecito, California

Dear Mr. Black,
This is Paulo writing to you. I am the one in the company that takes care of difficult/strange/desperate cases.

In addition, in my private life, I always do my best to surprise women and to get a woo-hoo reaction from them.

I am almost sure I am the person you are looking for to get the best out of this!

Now, I believe that a Bike tour of Tuscany could be the best way to get a great reaction from her, not getting any shoe thrown at you and to keep on looking tour leaders in their faces.

I must admit you have all my comprehension, as I know how hard it is to keep a woman by your side. Fortunately today you had a great Idea: you asked for a private bike tour trough Tuscany. This can definitely be the solution to your problems. Imagine to ride gently through the hills with a nice perfume of grapes mixed with the beauty of cypresses and chestnuts around you . . . Medieval Castles, old countryside churches and all the colors of the typical Tuscan landscapes. A glass of wine will all make it happier.

Imagine to be there with her, with a well-trained crew by your side, ready to pick you up when tired, ready to offer you soft drinks when thirsty, always at your disposal to eat when you are hungry . . .

No way to be disappointed . . .

Imagine your psychotherapist in the car reading the Montecito News . . . because not busy at all to make her smile . . . because there is not need when she is already smiling.

I promise, if you subscribe to our private bike tour, I will come myself, making sure everything will be perfect and no shoe will be thrown to anybody. I am by your side, Mark. Count on me.

Let me know if you wish to have a complete quote for a wonderful Private Tuscan Bike tour.

Have a great day, Mark!
Paulo

Dear Air New Zealand,

I have plans to lecture on Immanuel Kant in New Zealand, as has been my dream ever since I moved to Konigsberg. Given the philosophical nature of this journey, and my life in general, dietary considerations become paramount as I choose an airline to transport me.

I notice that you have a special meal that is labeled as bland. I believe that will work for me. But I also follow a gluten-free diet, which is an additional restriction. This is further complicated by the fact that I am lacto-ovo vegetarian, and I need to make sure that the meal is gluten free, as I am highly allergic to wheat.

I will be traveling with a fellow independent scholar from Saudi Arabia, a woman whom I hope to make my wife, so I must do everything I can to make sure she's satisfied fully. I bear the responsibility and burden of arranging her travels. She will require a Muslim meal, first of all. She is also a diabetic.

She has become rather overweight lately, and for this reason I will be asking for her to receive low-calorie meals as well, though I prefer that she not know that I made this portion of the request.

I would like to know how I should go about requesting the special meals, given these issues.

I would also like to know your policy regarding expressions of an amorous nature onboard. I can imagine that kissing is permitted, as well as some degree of necking. But am I wrong to assume that obvious displays are forbidden or are up to the discretion of your staff? I am traveling with a potential lover. Is the bathroom allowed for this purpose? Does it depend on the class of fare? We would love to have some guidelines for our behavior, as there seems to be some gray area.
Thank you,
Mark Black

Dear Mark,

Thank you for your recent request for a special meal to be provided on your Air New Zealand flights.

Air New Zealand currently offers 22 special meals options for our customers with religious, ethnic, and dietary requirements on our long-haul flights. If none of our special meals cover your medical requirements, you are welcome to bring your own suitable pre-packed meal on board with you. However, please remember that on all of our services, the aircraft facilities are not suitable for heating any meals you may bring with you. Also, we are unable to refrigerate your meals as they could become contaminated with other food items from the aircraft's refrigerators.

We realize that with severe food allergies, people can react to tiny traces of food inadvertently present in ingredients or on cooking utensils and sometimes even with tiny quantities of food in the air— the most common example is peanuts. As Air New Zealand's in-flight meals are prepared at over 20 kitchens around the world, it is not feasible to exclude these minute traces from the aircraft environment. Also, we cannot control what is brought onboard by other passengers or left behind by passengers from previous sectors. Therefore, we regrettably advise we are unable to provide allergen-free meals and/or an allergen-free environment on any of our flights.

If your allergy is severe, we strongly recommend you always carry appropriate medication onboard our services, in the event of a reaction. If you are not sure you will be able to administer your own medication in an emergency, we would advise you to travel with a companion who can assist you. Whilst our cabin crew are not permitted to administer medication, Air New Zealand does carry a comprehensive Physicians Kit on its jet services, and this is made available to any traveling doctor in a medical emergency. The kit does contain an "Epipen". In addition, we have specialist medical staff on call 24 hours a day to advise the crew on medical problems that may arise in flight.

In closing, we would like to reassure you that Air New Zealand is committed to ensuring your in-flight wellbeing and safety, and we hope you will understand our position on this matter.

If you don't want to be blacklisted from flying Air New Zealand, then I would refrain from using the bathrooms to "join the mile high club".

Keep your pants on till after you get off the flight, please.

Yours sincerely,

Dr. Eric Watson

Chief Medical Officer

Dear Germany Travel Services,
I have been reading everything to do with apodeictic philosophy since I attended lectures in the old days with your country's treasures, Habermas and Horkheimer. My hope has been to disprove the theory of *a priori* knowledge as explained by Immanuel Kant in Konigsberg a couple centuries ago. That has been my life's task.

Before that I was a luxury-products consultant for a firm in Saudi Arabia. Last week I purchased a map of Germany from Rand and McNally, and I have been scouring it up and down to find Kant's old town of Konigsberg.

I want to move there and finish my book on apodeictic knowledge. My German has gotten pretty good as a result of my inquiry. Can you please tell me where this town is? I ask my German friends, and they simply tell me to look at the map. I have no idea what's going on. I believe there is a castle there.

Also, if you happen to know the route of Kant's daily walk, that would be most helpful.
Viele Danke und Guten Tag,
Mark Black
Montecito, California

Dear Mr. Black,
Konigsberg used to belong to Prussia, but since WWII, it belongs to Russia, you will not find it on a current Germany map. Besides, the city was renamed Kaliningrad, so if you look for it on a map, do not look for Konigsberg. I cannot provide you with more information about Kaliningrad, please contact the tourist information of Russia or Kaliningrad itself.
Carl Friedrich
Deutsche Tourismus

Dear Switzerland Tourism Services,

I am thinking of coming to Switzerland on my way to Konigsberg, Germany, where I will be finishing my book on Immanuel Kant and absurdist knowledge.

I would like to know if Switzerland is boring or not. I've received mixed reports. I am told that it is beautiful, but I don't know if I will like it.

I am afraid of being bored. I will be reading many books about hermeneutics, and I plan on dining in because I eat only raw food and mostly citrus. I don't like trains and cars, so I plan on walking a lot. Don't worry, I'll bring the proper shoes.

I plan to buy nudist art while I am there, and I understand that there a number of great artists. I will meet them. I hope they're not boring.

Please let me know if you think I should come to Switzerland.

Thank you,

Mark Black

Dear Mark,

Greetings from Switzerland Tourism Services (Pvt.) Ltd! We recommend you to go to Switzerland if you are scenic lover and want to see nature. You have to go to Swiss if you love walk in ice . . . for art and artist we will recommend you to go for Italy tour package. Please suggest so that we can make and send you the package as per your taste.

Hope all are in order.

Please acknowledge receive of mail with your recommendation.

Thanks with best regards,

Devi Patel

Switzerland Tourism Services

Dear Platinum Star Private Jets,

I have need for a Gulfstream airplane starting this Monday, for four days. It requires the following itinerary: First pickup is in Bombay for my Saudi Arabian lover, who will be delivered to my house in Mallorca, Spain. I will give the pilot a 240 lb. package (I can't say what is in it) to be taken on the next flight, a pickup of my other lover in Latvia on the same day to be taken to New York City. My sister in Philadelphia will be meeting you at a designated airport, and she and her husband will need to be taken to a ribs joint in Nashville, Tennessee for an overnight stop. Then she will be flown to Las Vegas, where the two of them will spend the day gambling and doing a sixteen-course tasting menu at Robuchon, if you recommend that. Otherwise, perhaps the Ducasse restaurant? The next day (or as an overnight) those two plus five new women will board the flight to meet us in a remote location in Germany, where I will be giving a lecture on Sylvia Plath. I will not need a lift from Mallorca to Germany, unless you also have helicopters. The following day I will need you to fly me alone to be met at the runway by my other lover, in New York City.

Please let me know soon about how we can proceed.

Thank you,

Mark Black

Hi Mark,

Great. Lets work it out then. Can you please miss all the other details and only give me a clear breakdown of the journey in the following format: for each leg please put down: Origin Airport, Destination Airport, Date, Time, Number of passengers. Please inform if your priority is the budget of the trip or the trip itself. Do you want VIP configurations (more expensive)? Also, if the answer is budget, do give me an idea of the same for the full journey. We can certainly provide you just the right travel solution as per your requirement. A rough idea/budget is that this trip will certainly spill over into the million-dollar category. Package is fine. It should not be explosive or radioactive material. Rest is for you to get clearance at the customs in the US or Latvia wherever the package needs to be dropped.

Sincerely,

Satyam Sharma

Platinum Star Private Jets

CHAPTER TWO
MARK'S DINING NEEDS

Dear French Laundry Restaurant,

I know from experience how difficult it can be to secure a table at your renowned restaurant. My telephone has a calendar that allows me to book well into the future, so I was hoping you could make an exception for a young man who knows he would like to reserve a table for six for his sixtieth birthday meal on December 21, 2029. We would each like the full tasting menu and wine pairing. I don't know the dietary restrictions of those that will be present, but I can provide those as the date approaches.

Thank you,

Mark Black

Dear Mr. Black,

Thank you for e-mailing The French Laundry. While we appreciate your enthusiasm, unfortunately we are unable to secure reservations 19 years in advance. We are only able to make reservations up to two months to the calendar date in advance. Thank you for your patience, and we look forward to hearing back from you.

If we can be of any further assistance, please do not hesitate to let us know.

With our very best regards,

The French Laundry, Reservation Department

Dear Daniel Boulud and Mr. Vaidya, the Sommelier,
Daniel is quite a place. I have eaten at your illustrious restaurant
before, and my friends and I are considering coming in next month for
a birthday dinner. I am wondering whether you have any rare Kosher
wines in your cellar, particularly Manischewitz.

I'm not interested in doing pairings, or having the old cognacs this
time. I'm after that Friday night taste from childhood, to go along with
the chef's masterpieces. His cooking reminds me of the Provencal chef
my parents had when I was a boy. He learned to love Manischewitz
and thought it went particularly well with foods like sweetbreads. I'd
like to honor Pierre that night with a French song. Don't worry, I have
a great voice!

I look forward to hearing from you.
Sincerely,
Mark Black

D_ear Mr. Black,
Many thanks for your enquiry. We are delighted to learn that you will be returning to DANIEL this fall for a birthday dinner.

Regarding our wine cellar, while we certainly have the greatest respect for the traditions of every faith and culture, we regret that we do not have any kosher wines on our list. However, with over 1,500 selections available, we are confident we will be able to find a bottle to suit your tastes and your memories.

We look forward to welcoming you.

Georgette Farkas
Public Relations Director

Dear Stinking Rose Restaurant of Beverly Hills,
I am coming there with my ex-mother-in-law to celebrate a birthday. Not only did I not get to choose the restaurant, but they chose everything, including what color I'm supposed to wear.

They're an unusual bunch of people, but I guess I'm going to be OK, even though I'm not into it. Is it true that your restaurant specializes in garlic? I've been to the restaurant Website, and it does seem to be the case. I drove by on my way to Nobu and the street smelled like garlic. Interesting idea. I wish you luck. The thing is, I don't like garlic, and I don't eat garlic. When I travel I request the refugee diet on airplanes, because I can't handle garlic. I grew up vegan, but lately I've been more of a follower of the raw-food diet. I don't eat salad greens, though. Do you have something I can eat at your restaurant? If not, would you mind if I brought my own bowl of food. I'd be happy to give it to your plate presenters, so they could bring the meal that would look like it was something you made. I'm quite flexible and am interested in finding something that's easy. I don't know what I'm going to do about the odor of garlic, but maybe that night you can take it a little easy with the garlic.
Thank you,
Mark Black
Montecito, California

Hello Mark,

We definitely would like to help you have something that you can eat in our restaurant. Unfortunately our insurance does not allow us to have guests bringing their own food, but we still would like to accommodate your needs.

I have attached the link below that will take you to our menu. There are dishes that can be made without garlic, and they are marked with a vampire face/bat next to them. Please let me know if you find something that you can eat and then we will go from there.

Sincerely,

Rafael Santoro

General Manager

The Stinking Rose Restaurant

Beverly Hills, CA 90211

Dear Kogi Tacos,

Korean tacos? I stood in line for an hour with my identical twin while we were visiting California, and now we are betting a lot on your cuisine. I believe you can settle the matter. We are taking this seriously, and we have made a bet. I have a Brioni suit that he wants, and he has a green Ford Mustang from 1972 that I want. Your information will settle the matter, and my brother and I can put the matter behind us once we hear from you.

My understanding is that your tacos are Persian tacos, but he says that they are actually Lebanese tacos. I checked online, and it said something about the owner being Korean. I know they are not Korean tacos, but I can't figure it out. If they are Korean, then we will trade them for a six-month period. The cabbage in there is confusing me greatly.

Thank you and good day,

Mark Black

Konigsberg, Germany

Hi Mark,

Thanks for supporting us and coming out to try our food. That being said, if you both lose . . . do we get BOTH cars?!?!? Two of the three owners are Korean (me being one of them and the chef the other) and one is Filipino. Our food is Korean/Mexican, so not quite Lebanese or Persian. Sorry to disappoint you both.

If you'd like more information, we may be able to creatively make it work to be Persian . . . but I seriously think that it's a stretch. I wish you the best of luck on your bet!!

It looks like you might have to trade cars with your brother, because there is definitely a strong Korean influence in our food. Our chef considers it to be Angeleno food from a Korean perspective, but the combination of flavors are probably what have gotten you and your twin confused.

The two basic influences are Korean and Mexican. The corn tortillas are definitely a Mexican influence, while the marinated meats have a heavy Korean influence. Then we have our salsa roja, which combines Korean and Mexican and California chilies together, rounded off with a very Korean toasted sesame oil. Then there comes the salad, which is neither Korean nor Mexican, but is tossed in a LA-Korean chili-soy vinaigrette. And yes, there are shreds of cabbage tossed with romaine and green onion.

Ahahaha. I honestly don't know the difference between Persian and Lebanese food, so I have no idea which one it's more "like." However, maybe the construction of the taco can help you and your brother figure out whether it's MORE Persian or MORE Lebanese.

Love and tacos,

Alice and Caroline Shin

P.S. We're so flattered that you've written us from all the way in Germany! We hope you enjoyed your food. :)

Dear Animal Restaurant,
You have the best restaurant, the best chef, and the best ambiance in this city. I had the honor of having an endless tasting menu meal with my friend a few months back, and ever since I returned to Konigsberg, where I live, I have been telling my friends about your experiences offered. My summer home is in Montecito, but I live near Immanuel Kant's old house here in Germany.

I will be returning next month to check on my renovation of a glass pavilion for the Montecito home in about two weeks. Your chef is the best chef, and so I wonder if he would make me a special dish. It is my favorite dish in the world, and no one makes it like my grandmother did. It is called kaleh pocheh, and it is a sheep's head stew. The whole face is cooked. My grandmother learned it while she was in Iran, even though she isn't Iranian. She had a mysterious-sounding boyfriend there, and she would make it for him. I have been waiting ten years to ask a chef to make it for me, and now I give you that honor. But really the honor is mine. That would be part of the tasting menu I have in mind for my birthday meal. I will be there with one of my lovers, named Anke. She has been hearing about kaleh pocheh ever since we met in Saudi Arabia on business.
I look forward to hearing from you,
Mark Black

Hi Mark,

Thank you so much for your e-mail! Love your enthusiasm! At the moment we are in the process of opening another restaurant and will be unable to fulfill your request. I apologize, and good luck!!
Best,
Helen Johannesen

CHAPTER THREE
MARK'S QUIRKY NEEDS

Dear New York Colonics Center and Spa,
My colon has made me ecstatic for all the years I've graced the planet, but now I think it is time for me and my two lovers (from Brazil and Latvia) to sign up for a tune-up and finally take care of old business in a way that no enema can.

We have a few questions about colonics. Our preference is to have our colonics done simultaneously in the same room. My understanding is that there is some kind of plasma screen or television that shows exactly what is being released from the butt after each flush of liquid. I've heard of people videotaping those sessions and then studying them at a later date. That would be the other option, if we can't all get our colonics at the same time, in the same room. But it would be lovely if we could do that.

We are very close to one another, basically all the time. Inseparable. I installed a triple shower in my new master bathroom, and it has three Japanese toilets, three bidets, and three sinks. That's just to show you how we operate as a unit and why I am troubling you today.

We were so lucky to find one another that now there is no parting. It has been like this for almost eight years. I know, I'm lucky!

If we have to do the videotaping option, I wonder how far away from one another we will be. Is there a way that we will be in sight of one another, at least? We aren't co-dependent or anything. We just love being together.
I look forward to hearing from you,
Mark Black

Hello Mark,

I'm really happy that you feel lucky and that you have such a wonderful lifestyle and two lovers. Imagine that!

But unfortunately, we live in New York City and no such thing as a plasma TV in a colonic room exists yet.

And I don't know anybody who does colonics simultaneously for 2+ people. I'm so happy to have my center of vitality, but I treat my clients privately one on one.

But! . . . I'm open minded for you to videotape your lovers' colonic sessions, if you so wish and to be there (all 3 of you) during the whole process.

And you can study the videotapes in your leisure time. For 3 of you it will take about 3 hours and $150 each. $450 altogether (not including gratuity).

Hope to hear from you soon, and I hope that you will be able to "take care of old business" as only a good colonic can do.

—Helen

Dear Hermes,

I was recently in the Beverly Hills Hermes store, and I was thinking of purchasing a pair of socks. I know that this is a special label, as I've bought items for my lover when I traveled abroad (to make her happy), including three purses, and she bought me the $400.00 pair of boxers one Father's Day.

Our horses are groomed using only Hermes hoof-picks, and my grandchildren all carry Hermes muslin towels when they go sailing. My lover likes it that way, and I can't really complain. I almost bought the socks, because I love the way the H is placed just above the ankle. Whoever designed them is a maestro. But they are $55.00 and, I must confess, I am a miser. That doesn't mean I wouldn't buy such an item. I'm not trying to hoard my money, as some people suggest. I would buy a $55.00 pair of cotton socks, but I want to make sure that they are truly useful and comfortable for use over an entire day. I inquire today whether it is possible to purchase one sock. If I like the sock after a trial, I would buy the other one. I was told that I could return the socks if I bought the pair, but I don't think that would be fair. That's not how my mother raised me.

Thank you,
Mark Black
Montecito, California

Bonjour Mr. Black,
Thank you for visiting Hermes.com.

I apologize for any inconvenience, however we are unable to break up a pair of socks to sell them individually. We invite you to visit one of our boutiques to take a look at our socks if you are undecided. Again, thank you for your interest in Hermès. We look forward to your next visit with us. If you need additional information, please answer this message and keep the request reference [112428-128371086].

Best regards,

Ms. Petrova

Hermes Customer Service Department

Dear Bill's Car Armoring Service,

I have returned from a long stint in Latvia and would like to armor my new vehicle, a Smart Car. I know it is a tad small, but I find it to be the car that people are least drawn to shooting at. The people who might look for me won't look for such a silly car. They're thinking Maybach or Bentley. And at least the Smart Car is easy to park.

I am looking to get this car up to TAC ballistic level 7, so it can take a heavy beating if necessary. Handgun protection is insufficient. If you think that I will need to upgrade my car to something larger, please recommend the smallest car you think I could purchase for this purpose. I am an active environmentalist and believe strongly in lowering our carbon footprint.

Regards,

Mark Black

Montecito, California

H i Mark,

Thank you for contacting us and we appreciate your interest. Unfortunately, a Smart Car would not really be a suitable choice for armoring at any level—the vehicle is too weak in terms of horsepower and GVWR. For a level B6+, you will need to select a powerful vehicle (preferably an SUV or premium sedan) with a V8 engine. If level 7 is a must, I recommend going with a heavy duty SUV such as a Landcruiser/LX570 or Suburban/Yukon/Escalade. I understand that these vehicles may not fit in with your environmental views, but for armoring purposes a large, powerful vehicle is the most practical solution. If you have to choose between driving an environmentally friendly car and your life, I definitely recommend choosing the latter.

Please give me a call to discuss the project when you have a moment.

Take care,

Jason William Johnson

Bill's Armoring Service

Dear Accurate Wigs,

My girlfriend from Saudi Arabia is considering becoming Jewish once she comes to meet me and another "friend" in Latvia. She has a lot of hair, and she was wondering if she would be able to give you her hair so you could make a wig out of it. I told her that, if we get serious, I demand that she cut her hair, as I am sometimes Orthodox. But her hair is really beautiful. I am afraid it might still be sensual, even if it were a wig, but at least we would be following the rules God gave to us, at least as interpreted since the nineteenth century by Polish rabbi. She is willing to do this for me, because she thinks we have a bright and holy future together. I'm afraid to introduce her to my rabbi, but that's another story. She doesn't know that I have a house being built for her as we speak, near Gaza. Oh my, life is so complicated!

I look forward to hearing from you.

Mark Black

(in London right now)

D_{ear} Mark,

I don't know how much I can help you with your relationship, but I can tell you that we do buy hair sometimes from people. Your girlfriend would have to come to us. As she lives in Saudi Arabia, I can see that would be a problem. Now, as to making a wig from her hair. First of all, it takes more than one head of hair to make a full wig. Second of all, if you want to make a wig (sheitel, parik) for her to cover her hair, it would depend on the rabbi you ask. This is a question that has come up to us before. We are wigmakers, not rabbis. We have heard from our customers different answers from different rabbis. Some forbid it completely, some allow it, and some say you can use the hair only in the back of the wig.

Good luck with everything.

Candy

Production Manager

Accurate Wigs

Dear POM Juice Customer Service,

I drink your pure pomegranate juice three times a day, each time after walking three miles at three miles per hour. I take the same route, just as Emmanuel Kant did. But I'm not in Konigsberg. He's my hero. So are Marguerite Duras and Botticelli. The later work of Hemingway is up there. Sorry to wander, but I'm so excited to be writing you. I love you guys! I've learned from my neighbor, a food chemist and all-around genius, that walking that pace opens up my taste buds. Needless to say, I eat a lot of fresh pomegranates during the season, before I go for the walk, of course. Each one tastes different, but when I drink your POM juice it always tastes exactly the same. I'm confused. Is it me, or is it the drink? I don't understand how it is possible, mathematically. I realize one plus one equals two, but you guys are making millions of bottles of this elixir for other people just like me, and we're all grateful. Is it me, or are my taste buds fooling me, even though I'm going three miles per hour?

Mark Black

Montecito, California

Dear Mr. Black,

Thank you for contacting us with your intriguing inquiry. We do our best to make POM Juice consistently flavorful. We grow only Wonderful variety pomegranates in California. The fruit is hand-picked and then juiced in our plant. We control the process of production from tree to bottle, so we can only surmise that the flavor is very constant. We are pleased to hear that you enjoy pomegranates, and we hope you will be seeing our fresh poms in stores in about a month. Keep up the good work with walking and reading the classics. It is great to keep the body and mind in peak condition!

Healthy Wishes,

P♥M Wonderful

Consumer Affairs

Dear Spinelli Private Investigation,

I need help. I have a lover who is from Saudi Arabia and another lover who lives in Germany. I live outside Santa Barbara. I believe they are going to be meeting each other. Each of them could be married. It is a total mess.

I am not married, but my ex-wife, who lives in New Jersey, has been reading my e-mails and she is furious that I have these women in my life. I told her that I was leaving her for other reasons (gay, etc.). That was two months ago.

I would like to hire an investigator to follow one of the women. I'm not sure where you travel or have agents, but I need someone to follow either the one in Germany or the one in Saudi Arabia. The one in Saudi Arabia is brilliant. She is in Mensa, and she's a total fireball.

I will need your person to cause interference if he knows she is heading to the airport in Saudi Arabia. I will pay for this, should it arise. I cannot have a meeting between these three women, in case my ex-wife shows up too. I would prefer that you send a woman, but would not object were it a man. The person has to know how to drive quickly, because both these women are rather crazy drivers.

Thank you,

Mark Black

D ear Mr. Black,
This case would require a huge retainer, we do not work on cases and then bill, this is against company policy, anywhere from $50,000.00 to $100,000.00 would be required for us to undertake this case.
Respectfully,
Peter Franco Spinelli

Dear Executive Limousine of NYC,

I am curious about your availability for the following request. The vehicle need not be a Rolls Royce, except perhaps on the final day when a marriage may take place. As long as it is clean, I will be satisfied. I will be doing an advance pay for a specific job. The timing and secrecy are what is paramount. At 2:11 a.m. each day between October 18 and October 26, I need to have a small woman of mine picked up at the same location in front of a complex on lower Fifth Avenue near Washington Square Park and taken to an apartment to be specified on West Twenty-First Street. That's all it is. She will always be wearing white. The job is a safe one, but requires absolute privacy. There is no need for an armored car. Then, at 4:20 a.m., she and I would be transported to a warehouse in Hell's Kitchen. Nothing else will be needed on that morning. I would like to know if you are able to handle this request and would like a rough idea of the price.

Sincerely,

Mark Black

Good Evening Mr. Black,

Thank you for contacting Executive Limousine. Based on the information provided, we are accustomed to detailed itineraries and requests. We provide a very wide range of vehicles from Rolls Royces to Lincoln Town Executive L sedans. I would suggest one of our late model Black Mercedes S550 to accommodate your itinerary. The vehicle is luxurious and low profile compared to a Rolls Royce. Our standard rate is $95 an hour, plus gratuities, fees, and sales tax. We will provide the same driver for each evening to assure the highest quality of service. Is this something you would be interested in?

Please feel free to contact me directly. I look forward to hearing from you!

Best Regards,

Franco Montenegro

D ear David Ranter Real Estate,

I remember you. Your name would be seen often when I lived in the Palisades, and now I live further north, but I miss life down there. My hope is to find the cheapest house that is closest to the old home of Nicole Brown Simpson, on Bundy, where the whole mess went down.

I am a historian by education and plan on walking back and forth between her home, O.J. Simpson's home on Rockingham, and the old restaurant where she dined. I will be driving it and walking it repeatedly, as part of a larger project.

The nature of that project is rather private, but I can assure you that it is fascinating. I suppose anywhere on these routes is OK, but being steps away from her old place would be the ideal. However, my budget for both the home and this poetic investigation is severely limited, due to an incident with one of my lovers in Germany, where I also keep a simple home under a castle. All I need is a bedroom and bathroom. No kitchen is necessary. My budget is roughly 1.5 million, give or take 800,000 or so. The more I save on the housing, the more I can use for my investigation.

My tastes are rather Germanic and Spanish when it comes to aesthetics. As I said, the most important thing is finding something on that route.

For that I would be grateful. I look forward to hearing from you. I plan on coming down to your area within six days.

Thank you,

Mark Black

Montecito, California

Dear Mark,

Thanks so much for your request. We too found the entire O.J. situation to be fascinating and wondered if the full story would ever be known. I would have responded sooner, but was on the east coast this weekend and just returned to catch up with e-mails. Jolie has been with me for 16+ years and specializes in identifying ideal home solutions for buyers in the Palisades, Brentwood, and Santa Monica. She'll do the research and get back to you as soon as we can. I am confident that in that price range we will have alternatives for your consideration!

Thanks again for the opportunity to be of service.

David Ranter

Pacific Palisades, California

Dear Jaguar Corporation,

I am interested in purchasing a new Jaguar with the steering wheel on the left and right sides. Ideally, it could be removable on one side, so that a passenger would not be responsible for driving. I hope to buy several vehicles over time because I am starting a luxury car learning school in Montecito. I plan to have Ferraris and similar cars as well. My philosophy is that people want the best. Jaguar has always been a pretty great car, even now, despite the reputation for it being a clunker. Please let me know if this is possible.

Thank you,

Mark Black

Dear Mark Black,

Thank you for contacting the Jaguar Customer Relationship Center. We appreciate your inquiry. At this time Jaguar Cars does not have a vehicle which has this feature. We apologize for any inconvenience this may cause. If you have any questions or require additional information, please feel free to contact us at 1-800-4-JAGUAR, option 9.

Regards,

Hilde Gollen

Jaguar Customer Service

Dear Walt Disney Concert Hall,
I am in a predicament. It is almost a quagmire. For over twenty years
I've been going to Saudi Arabia for one reason, a very short woman
that I am in love with. She has slammed every door in my face and has
told me that she won't love me back. The story would make anyone
weep, as I've been through so much, emotionally and physically. It isn't
easy going to Saudi Arabia every month for so many years, each time
carrying my cello all the way there. I practice every day and I play for
her. She is my muse. This is where your facility comes in. I told her
that I have been invited to play at your notable hall.

I know, I lied to her. Trust me, I had no choice.

She's suddenly interested in coming back to America with me. I
wonder if I can book a room for a concert somewhere in your hall. It
wouldn't have to be the main hall. I assume you have multiple venues
in your large building. This way she will not hurt me for having lied
to her.

Please let me know if there is anything we can work out. I have
become desperate.
Regards,
Mark Black
Montecito, California

Dear Mr. Black,

Thank you for your inquiry and your patience. You might want to consider renting BP Hall at the Walt Disney Concert Hall. To do so, please contact Harry Diamond, in charge of booking.

Thank you for your time, attention, and support.

Sincerely,

Los Angeles Philharmonic Information

Dear Michael Thompson of the International Rock Paper Scissors Society,

I have a question about a variation on RPS which I learned while I was traveling last year in northern Iran, near the Iraqi border. I am a consultant on cows, so they brought me in for that purpose. Anyway, they add a fourth possibility, which is a snake. A snake can eat paper, but would die with a rock or scissors. It entertained us a great deal. The symbol for it is stretching out your index finger. They call it snake rock paper scissors. I've tried playing it here in Germany with my friends when we have our monthly bratwurst gathering, and if we start before we drink too much beer then they find the game fantastic. Once they are drunk they forget about the snake. My thought is that children who learn the snake game would be able to play it even when they are drunk. Anyway, I'd love to sponsor a tournament here in Konigsberg at my home, which is beneath the castle. It would be a lovely setting for the world's best players. Would you be interested?

Warm regards,

Mark Black

Konigsberg, Germany

H i Mark,
I must say Cow Consultant is a new job title in my experience. The "snake" addition to the game is like a whole bunch of similar fourth elements to the game. While interesting, it actually ruins the balance of the game, since now there are throws that win and lose unequally to others. Refer to the Myth of Dynamite Exposed on our site for more on fourth elements.

If you are serious about running a tournament, we could certainly discuss, but a few questions first:

What kind of prize are you looking to give? How many people will you be able to hold? Do you have sponsors lined up? Please let me know, and we can discuss further.

Cheers,
Michael Thompson
Managing Director, International RPS, Inc.

Dear Authentic Capes,
I have spent the last three hours looking at capes on the Internet,
and I must say you make the finest capes I've ever seen. The entire
medieval world would envy your product. I didn't realize there were
others like me who had this love. I've been making my own jouster-
type capes ever since I was a kid, and our whole family would make
them at Christmas time. Your choice of tagua nuts shows me you
know your stuff. We had tagua trees at our place in Hawaii, and most
of my buttons throughout my childhood came from that tree in the
backyard.

Regarding my order, I wonder if you would make capes in pure
cashmere? I don't like any other fabric anymore. I itch like you don't
want to know with everything else. I can supply you with the cashmere,
if you don't have it. I have a roll of it in my attic that I brought back
with me from Italy on the *Queen Mary* last year. I was going to have a
suit made, but decided against it. Now that I see your capes, I figure
my family could use them. I've got four kids and nine grandchildren.
It might be too much in terms of costs, but I thought I'd throw it out
there. You never know. I might even fly in and help out!

I look forward to hearing from you.
Mark Black

Dear Mark,
Sorry, but at this time we are unable to fulfill your request. Thanx for considering us.
Nelly, Authentic

CHAPTER FOUR
MARK'S INTELLECTUAL NEEDS

Dear Peter Max,

I would like to buy a painting from Peter Max himself. I never buy a painting unless the painter himself gives it to me. I don't need to speak to the painter, and I don't need to do anything other than have the painter hand me the painting. I do not mind if the painting is already signed, and I do not need to videotape the exchange. If you would prefer that a lawyer be present, then that is a preference I would honor. My sole concern when purchasing a painting is this, once I decide that I want to buy a painting from a particular painter. I am convinced that this is the right choice for my collection and am planning on being in the USA within two weeks, if I can sort out some of my business here in Stockholm.

Please let me know how you would like to proceed.

Thank you,

Mark Black

D̲ear Mr. Black,

Thank you for your interest in collecting Peter Max. Can you tell me what you're interested in? I would be happy to sell you a painting and have Peter Max hand it to you at our studio in New York.

Best regards,

David Murray

Sent via BlackBerry by AT&T

Dear Vito Acconci,

I have an issue that I believe only you can resolve. For twenty-two years I have been pursuing a Saudi Arabian woman named Fatimah. She is the love of my life, but she abuses me. I have made 238 visits to Riyadh, where she lives, and each time I've come home without her. When Fatimah was a teenager hoping to become an artist she started watching your strange movie *Seedbed* on a daily basis. Her father tried stealing the videotape from her, but she would find a copy somehow. Her uncle believes that she knew some powerful people in the black market in Yemen or Stockholm. They told me that she would never be with me, that she is in love with you. I don't know what to say. I've watched that video where you are masturbating but I don't understand it. I'm a simple person.

My thought is that maybe she would come with me to live if I were to promise her that I could arrange for her to meet you. This would be an opportunity to meet one of your biggest fans. Would this be possible? I promise to make it brief and non-sexual, of course. I think once she meets you in person she may lose the obsessive aspect of her love and begin to let herself open to me. That is my theory.

I would hope that you would do your best not to do something that would further seduce her. She is rather suggestible for some reason. But I love that little woman more than anything in the world!
Regards,
Mark Black

M̲ark Black,

Please excuse my delayed answer; I admit, I avoided answering. I understand your plight—at least as much as I can understand from afar & from a brief description. I wish your situation could change & that you could get what you want. I wish that what she wants & what you want could come closer together. But I can't find for myself a good reason for me to get involved in this . . .

Vito Acconci

Dear Alain de Botton,

If you only knew how much Heidegger I read, you'd feel sorry for the fact that I still don't know anything about being. Add to that all the malaise because of having been rejected by everyone all my life, most notably women. Philosophy means nothing if I can't find love. Love means nothing if I can't express happiness. Joy means nothing if all it adds up to is a pile of notes written to myself, scribblings toward a world that will never exist and that always recurs.

Why write you? I know you're asking this about now, and I can understand the sentiment. You're wise. Or you sound wise. I try not to be. If I could I would do nothing with my life. If I could turn into a pelican tomorrow, I would. But the real problem is that I am still the kind of person who reads biographies of Balzac to find a clue to how I should live. If I were more like you, maybe I would have something at this point to speak for. Perhaps at the root of my suffering is the sorrow I feel when I walk past a tin of beluga caviar and I know I can't buy it, because I devoted my life to this wretched path of self-reflection. I end up with anchovies, on a good day. Otherwise it is lentils. How pathetic. Champagne doesn't go with legumes. Besides, I was born for more. I protest at my circumstances. There has to be a better way. I've read all your books. You must work around the clock to keep up with yourself. Please continue doing so.

Mark Black

Dear Mark,

I share your thoughts and doubts and pains. Reading Heidegger is an ambiguous benefit.

Have you tried psychotherapy? I recently restarted, and it's just fantastic, the only thing that can help. I will write about it all one day.

Thank you so much for reading my stuff—and I send you my good wishes, though life is dark, of course.

Alain

Dear Mr. Bleckner,

While expanding my modern collection at a slow rate I have wondered for a while if I should purchase a work of yours. I have a friend who likes it a great deal, and we go back and forth about it.

I went to your Website, because I don't like galleries and I was immediately attracted to all the childish renderings of marbles. They're quite something. You must be proud. If I had to choose one, it would be the one that has lots of yellow marbles. You call it Mysticism for Beginners. I happen to despise mysticism, considering it to be the number one problem in the world. I told my friend that, and, though he agrees with me, he thinks that shouldn't interfere with an appreciation of the simple painting. I feel so young when I look at it. I wonder what you had in mind when you made it and if you wanted us to feel something like this. I read a lot of Dr. Seuss when I was young, and I think he's helpful. My question to you is about the title. If I were to purchase it, would you be willing to change the title?

I look forward to hearing from you.

Regards,

Mark Black

Montecito, California

M ark,

I don't like mysticism either . . . I liked the title. If you look at my Website, rbleckner.com, you'll see that those paintings are actually paintings that have to do with forming and unforming . . . things in the body (fragility), DNA strands, molecules. Viruses, some of which we understand, most of which we don't . . . the painting you are referring to was sold long ago, as are all of the others on the Website. It is not a sales Website, just information. I do appreciate your interest. ross b

Mr. Bleckner,

I appreciate your response and am glad we share the dislike. You must be quite a mensch to sell everything there. Bravo! My life feels like one long forming and reforming.

A general question then—when you sell a painting, would you change the name if that were an issue? I have a problem in that, when I buy paintings, I can't have the original name.

Regards,

Mark

Dear Mark,
lol, that's a funny question, very hypothetical, since it never comes up. I guess I'd change the name, I like a painting to have a relationship outside of the meaning(s) I assign to it . . . sometimes other people have better ideas about an artists work than the artist.

D_{ear} Mr. Bleckner,

That's a modest response, and I'm relieved to see that you have a fluid relationship to the work.

Thank you,

Mark Black

Dear Majida, the Belly Dancer,
I had the good fortune of seeing you dance when I was in your country, and I believe you are excellent, and was wondering about your schedule this fall, because I am having a special party and would like to discuss inviting you. I live in Konigsberg, Germany, next door to a castle where my fiancée, a second cousin, has lived since she was a child. I will be moving into the castle with her after we get married. I can hardly wait for that night. My future wife would like to know if you would be willing to dance for us on our wedding night. She is the love of my life, really. It would be an appropriate invitation as we continue on our journey as a united person.

The spirit of Arabia in Germany while it is maybe snowing would be nearly mystical. We are not mystical, but this would be a special feeling in the castle, you, your red hair, the music. We could have music playing. I was thinking of bringing a band from my friend's village in central Anatolia. He knows a saxophonist or clarinetist, I forget which, but I know he plays microtones. I believe the whole experience will take about thirty minutes to seven hours maximum duration, depending on your endurance.
I look forward to your answer,
Mark Black

Hi there Mark,
Majida has engagements in North America November 11–16 and November 19–21. So that time frame probably would not work. It's a bit of an unusual request to have a show for just two people, so unless it is in a public place or Majida is there with her road manager, I'm not sure if it would work. Nevertheless, if you have more details, or a different date frame, please feel free to contact us again.
Best regards,
Raqsie

Dear Steven Reich,
My son is having a Bar Mitzvah in June, and we were wondering if you would be willing to play your music.

There will be no dancing, and I expect there to be many in the audience who will be expecting something else, so I thought the avant garde Mr. Reich would enjoy that. My son is a curious fellow, having decided at age 44 to convert to Judaism and get a Bar Mitzvah, but that's another story. If Mr. Reich likes caviar there will be an unusually high amount of it at the party, because my son is one of the foremost importers of the stuff from the Caspian. That and backgammon boards from Turkey. The location: We are still deciding whether to have it in Dubai or in Beirut. My lover is from Saudi Arabia, and she knows those countries well and she feels that the quality of party and cuisine will be higher there than anywhere else.

I would like to have it at the Riverdale Yacht Club in New York. I don't know if I will get away with that.

That's enough about the party, and us. I can tell you more down the road. Budget is not an issue, so long as we come up with a fair price. I realize the historical importance of Mr. Reich as a composer.
Warm regards,
Mark Black

Dear Mr. Black,

Steve asked me to send a *mazal tov* on the forthcoming Bar Mitzvah. He no longer performs. If you are interested in a performance of Reich's works I can suggest some excellent local ensembles.

Yours,

Howard Stokar

Howard Stokar Management

Hi Ms. Metaphor,

Your site is full of wisdom, like you say. My question concerns my inner world. I like poetry, but absolutely detest poets. When I consider a poem, I can't bear to think of the poet. It is even worse if I know the poet. Usually they don't bathe enough, and they don't study themselves. They act like beaten-up animals. Not all poets, but I mean the poets that I've met. I don't want to share my inner world with them. No. Not one moment of my life. I have a garden of delights to walk through, full of cherry and mulberry trees. Do you understand that? Children play nearby, even. That gives me solace. So does my hybrid. My inner world is a quiet place. It can't be sacrificed. They sacrifice themselves constantly. That's my observation. If they read the poem to me it is even worse. Do you like poetry readings? I get crazy. I've known many poets in my long life. I want them to be quiet. I want them to stop writing. Words, words, words, all over everything. They aren't Emily Dickinson, even though they think they are. I feel bad even talking about this. It raises my sensitivity. I feel like Sylvia Plath meets Mishima.

I look forward to hearing your advice. Maybe you can tell me how to handle this. Please don't recommend an immersion.

Thank you,

Mark Black

Montecito, CA

M r. Black,

Perhaps you, like the poet Mark Strand, need to vary your diet:

> Ink runs from the corners of my mouth. There is no happiness
> like mine.
> I have been eating poetry . . .

Your innards and inner world are apparently quite sensitive to gastric poetic-distress. It is simple enough to avoid the Many Poets, along with the ensuing heartburn. Just don't go there, wherever they are. However, Ms. Metaphor wouldn't want to see you develop metrophobia. It's best to take a homeopathic dose of a Bad Poet now and again, just so you don't break into a rash if you run into a barefoot bard at the park. But don't get gloomy and lose your appetite over dead poets. Handle it with a lighter touch:

> We sat together at one summer's end,
> That beautiful mild woman, your close friend,
> And you and I, and talked of poetry.
> I said, "A line will take us hours maybe;
> Yet if it does not seem a moment's thought,
> Our stitching and unstitching has been
> naught . . .
> W. B. Yeats, from Adam's Curse

MS. Metaphor

Dear Gagosian Gallery,

On my way back home to Saudi Arabia, I made sure to stop in New York and see the Damien Hirst show, at the behest of my dear friend in Connecticut, who believes I should add one of those pieces to my collection. I'm not convinced, and have never thought much of Mr. Hirst's artwork. In your space everything looks like art. That's what is so special about your concept.

The bull's head in a frame is a nifty idea, I guess, and though I am skeptical of the merit, my friend keeps reminding me that this isn't only about my ideas on art, but that this is an investment. I've met Mr. Hirst at a fundraiser in London, and I didn't have the heart to give him my opinion of his work. Usually it is better to keep this to oneself. If I've learned anything from my wiser friends, it is that I should keep my opinions to myself. I'm not sure why my friend is so insistent about me owning one of those pieces. He e-mailed me this morning and reminded me that this is the right time to consider such an investment. That is my way of asking whether that piece with the carcass is still available.

Sincerely,

Mark Black

Dear Mark,

I hope this e-mail finds you well. I'm writing to introduce myself and follow up on your inquiries below regarding Damien Hirst. Please feel free to call me directly at the gallery at your earliest convenience to discuss further. I look forward to speaking with you. The work you're referring to, "End of an Era," was sold some time ago. I can send images of additional vitrine sculptures by Damien if interested. We have a few great ones available for you to consider. Please let me know.

Best,

Ron, Sent via BlackBerry from T-Mobile

Dear Kevin Ridgway:
I've read all your books, even the ones I've found that are supposedly not written by you, though my friend says they are, and I've loved them, so thank you. That's why I'm choosing you to ask if you'd write a letter for me. Thus begins the story. You see, I have a link to your homeland, too, but it involves a complex association through a woman I'd met named Desiree, a school teacher who lives in Los Olivos, California, where I had my vineyard. In mid-June of 1988, I had been sitting under an olive tree, when Desiree pulled up in her Sedan de Ville and asked me for directions to the local spa. I invited her inside for a salad of fresh garbanzo beans. She was shocked, because she'd once been married to a certain Martin Cruz of the Philippines, and he had been a garbanzo farmer. In September of 1993 I had been in Dublin promoting my wine for a luxury consultancy company run out of Riyadh, and lo and behold, I'd met Mr. Cruz at the same foodie festival that I'd been invited to address. Somehow we got to talking about Desiree, and he'd told me that they'd never been married. He claims that he'd been married to Desiree's sister, who had died while traveling in India. By this time I had been not so happily married to Desiree for almost six years. Not until March of 2001 did I discover, with the help of a private investigator, that she'd been married to a man in Chinatown in New York City. This gentleman owns a fish market to this day. Whenever I am in NYC I walk by his stinky shop, and I wonder what on earth she could ever have seen in him. Anyway, I would like to write him a letter to find out why he divorced Desiree.

It is 2011, and I am thinking about following in his footsteps, but I can't do it without knowing why he did it. I thought you might have a clue about how I can go about this, and perhaps do it for me.
Your fan,
Mark Black

Hi Mark,

Why don't you just write a very simple letter asking the stinky fish shop man why he divorced Desiree? I can't do it for you. I am not good with that sort of thing. Did you confront Desiree about the contradictions between her story and that of Martin Cruz? Do you still own the vineyard? What are garbanzo beans? Why don't you just go into the stinky shop and ask the man about his relationship with Desiree? Why not just ask Desiree? Why did you hire a private investigator? Is your wine business a success?

I wish you all the best with these complications. I am only sorry that fiction is, when it comes to the practical arrangements of life, completely useless.

K

Dear Alex Grey,
I have a collection of modern art, including works by Taaffe, Twombly, and Richter. My friend, actually my masseuse, suggested I take a look at your work. I deplore the new age, as well as anything that has to do with eastern mysticism. That's the worst thing that has ever happened to art or New York City. It is as if the Buddha set up camp in the Village and won't leave. But I feel like your work is more physical. I feel like it isn't spiritual. I feel like it might be seen as essential and humorous. I don't see how it can't be metaphysical. If I live with it, I wonder how it will affect me. That's important, you know. But I think I'm not sure about it. I have another friend who told me not to buy anything of yours, but I want to disagree with him. He and I disagree about neckties also. Perhaps you can tell me whether you think this is a good idea, purchasing something. Or do you think I'll regret it?
Thank you,
Mark Black

D ear Mark,

Thanks for writing with candor.

Alex and I both feel that you will regret it. Yes, the work is metaphysical. Yes, it is influenced by science, particularly anatomy and chemistry. It is also distinctly spiritual and influenced by Eastern and Western Mysticism. Collectors of Alex's art are independent thinkers that do not follow standard art marketplace recommendations. Check out alexgrey.com and cosm.org. CoSM is the organization we co-founded, and it has it's home in the Hudson Valley near Beacon (Dia Beacon). You are welcome to visit our studio there.

Best wishes,

Allyson Grey

Dear Sparrow, the Poet,
I attended one of your poetry readings years ago at the Poetry Project, and I was moved by your words and by your long, holy beard.

I am not a poet. I run a luxury consultant company in Saudi Arabia. But I don't care for my name. I have been thinking of changing my name to Finch.

I realized this week that I should ask you, of all people, whether you recommend the change.
Warm Regards,
Mark Black (Finch)

Mark:

I appreciate your tenacity. Thanks for trying twice! Is that what a finch would do? I know very little about birds, even sparrows. Though lately I'm reading a book by William Carlos Williams, in which he has a famous poem about the sparrow. Which contains lots of disturbing news about my species.

As for the finch, I doubt that I can help you decide whether to take its name.

I don't especially like the name Sparrow, but neither am I planning to change it. Very often a young, good-looking woman tells me how much she loves my name. It is a name for women to love, not for me.

But thank you for your flattery of my poetry and beard. It sounds like you want to name yourself Finch, and are just awaiting my approval. If that is the case, my approval is yours.

Predictively,

Sparrow

CHAPTER FIVE
MARK'S NUDIST NEEDS

Dear Ostrich Farm,
I am the head planner for a group of theoretical scholars from around the world (but mostly the Ivory Coast and Sweden) who gather once a year in exotic locales.

This year we've chosen New Zealand. We are comprised of approximately 400 nudists, sometimes 500.

Someone suggested we contact you about arranging either for a ride or for an ostrich race. We would, of course, be without clothing.

Some people take issue with that, but we feel it is the natural way, of course. We are not a sexual group of any kind.

I see that you have a wine shop as well, so perhaps we could have a combination wine tasting, meal, and ostrich race. In the past, the staff of facilities that have welcomed us have each done their own thing. Some joined us, some have worn only slippers, while others were fully clothed.

I would like to know if you think that riding the ostrich in the nude will hurt. We are planning this event for April of 2011.
I look forward to hearing from you,
Mark Black

Hi Mark,

We do not do racing. The ostrich riding is part of our guided ostrich tour. It takes place at the end of the tour and approximately 10% of the group can ride. We also have a weight limit of 75kg.

We take approximately 50 pax out per tour.

Yes, it is possible to ride naked. We do have a denim type of saddle which the ostriches wear. The denim material covers the back of the ostrich . . . where the people sit on . . .

That should be enough protection.

Kind regards,

Tanya, Yarden Ostrich Farm

Dear Jiraffe Restaurant:

I dined in your restaurant the last time I was in the USA. That was two years ago. It was fantastic. I still remember the shining example of your foie gras with mangoes and that simple chocolate cake.

I'm writing you today because a group of us is visiting Santa Monica in December, and we wondering if your restaurant would allow us to rent your whole place for an international event. We are mostly a group of elderly German and Scandinavian nudists who meet in one place annually.

This year we chose your township. We are a civilized group, even though we like to eat without clothing. Your servers would be welcome to be clothed, if that is their preference. We prefer they don't. Please let me know whether your restaurant would consider this option.

Sincerely,

Mark Black

Königsberg, Deutschland

M~ark,~

We did not see this until just now, we do apologize. Entertaining your guests in such circumstances is not something we can accommodate.

Thank you for your inquiry.

Jiraffe Restaurant

Dear Firenze Trattoria,

The members of our nudist organization have chosen your restaurant to cater our next annual convention in Chicago this winter, given that the restaurateurs in California are so close-minded and won't let us come there. We had our last gathering in Beirut, where we made falafel, but the one before was making pizzas in Roma. That was a success. We are avid cooks and foodies, with many fascinating members, from African and Scandinavian countries, predominantly. We are not into sadism or anything like that. This is our first gathering in America, and we hope to branch out with new people while there. Yours is a large restaurant, so I am not sure if roughly 400 people is enough to close the restaurant for a night as a private party. If so, we would like to have the event there. If not, I was told about a large loft space in the Korean Meat Packing District. We would be renting a few ping-pong tables as well.

We are quite militant about being clothingless at our gatherings, so we would expect the servers to be nude as well. We don't mind the use of light colored slippers, given that they'll be doing a lot of walking. One year we had a paella event in Valencia, and the waiters wore tennis shoes. They looked ridiculous.

Please let us know if you are available for private bookings and what we need to do on our end to secure your services.

Sincerely,

Mark Black

Konigsberg, Germany

Mark,

Thanks for thinking of Firenze as your next gathering while in Chicago. Unfortunately, this is not an event that Firenze would be able to take part in. We appreciate your thinking of us.

Sincerely yours,

Robbie Pearce

Director of Operations, Firenze Trattoria

Dear Mandarin Concierges,

My friend and I are planning on visiting China in a month. We have several goals, but are a bit concerned about achieving them in the three short weeks when we will be in Shanghai. First of all, we would like to rent an apartment that does not have a kitchen. We would like to have a catered meal of dog meat in our room. I understand that this is possible, but I want to make certain that it is possible. I keep kosher usually and, for that reason, am not able to eat at most restaurants.

I travel with my own plates and table service. I do not have a chef with me, however. Before the meal we plan to visit the best spa and receive a full treatment. For me it is difficult to take time off work because my boss is such an impossible person, but I want to make this the trip of a lifetime.

I thought your service would make it possible and efficient to satisfy my various requirements. I would like to travel by horse and buggy through Shanghai, rather than by car. I wonder if it is possible to be picked up at the airport this way. If this is not possible, then I would like for it to be available to me in the center city.

Additionally, we plan to have at least four women with us at all times. That is the correct impression that I wish to make while visiting China. That may require more women, because I don't sleep but three hours a night, so I imagine we would have to hire more. We will need a tailor to handle our clothing requirements, but we will be spending at least 20% of our times in a spa without clothes on. If a full-time concierge is your recommendation, I would be open to discussing hiring one. I have many more specific wishes for the trip, but will politely ask if we can wait to communicate those until after I hear your suggestions.

Kindly,

Mark Black

Germany

Dear Mr. Black,
Thank you for considering China Concierge.

We understand all of your requirements from your e-mail, unfortunately, we won't be able to arrange you the trip you desire. First, we don't rent apartments for our clients, we can only book hotels for them.

Second, we only provide private van services. And, horses are not allowed on the road in China.

Third, we cannot arrange you women except female tour guides, whose main job is to take you to places of interests and explain the history for you. We apologize for not being able to provide you the tour again.

Sincerely yours,
Mia Jin, Mandarin Concierges

Dear Yoga Training Camp,

I have been a yoga student for some time now, learning from a small woman I met in Saudi Arabia, mostly. Very little else in my life makes me happy, so I have decided to devote my life to sharing my love for yoga with the world. I would like to open a yoga center one day. The Mark Black Center for Total Divinity and Mind-Body Enlightenment, headquartered in Saudi Arabia or Beirut. Your one-stop shop for all things perfect in the world. But I need to become certified as a teacher. My friends suggested I contact your organization. My yoga center will be clothing optional. I hope to have a raw-food, vegan restaurant attached to it. The location will be somewhere in the Middle East, because my lovers are there. Plus, it is hot there, and I only like doing yoga in musty rooms. There is a special feeling in the Middle East, a certain vibration. You get it when in Mother India too, or that's what Fatimah says. But India is too dirty for me. Plus I only want to be around spiritual seekers, and India is full of people who only care about money. Next to the restaurant, I hope to build a temple for all the religions, but especially Buddhism and Hinduism, maybe some Kabbalah-style Judaism. It will be a shrine for all those seeking perfection of spirit. Please let me know about what level of commitment is required to receive certification and when your next training begins.

Devotedly,

Mark Black

Hi Mark,
Namaste! I like your ideas about the raw-food restaurant with the open-religion temple adjoining your yoga studio. It has a uniqueness to it. The one thing that causes some hesitation is the clothing optional. It sounds beautiful, it goes with the idea of open spirituality, but may bring a certain crowd. It might limit the type of people coming. Thank you for correctly informing me about the openness of the people in the Middle East. I also like the idea of a Divine Love yoga center. It sounds beautiful. Many blessings! The name sounds good. I like the one-stop shop. Send us your contact information when you're up and running.

Are you planning on offering retreats, or is it more like an ashram, where people come to study and live? Or just daily yoga classes? If you found the right target group, I think your ideas for the yoga center could be successful. I hope my opinion has given you some insight.

Please contact us if you have any other questions.

Many blessings! Sweet dreams!

Fellow Yogini,

Shanti Smith

CHAPTER SIX
MARK'S SEXUAL NEEDS

D̲ear Tantrist,

I have been looking up the word tantra day and night, ever since I came back from Latvia, where I met a new lover who joined me with my Brazilian lover. She is always talking about tantra. It was rather awkward because, in the midst of our early-morning, good-bye lovemaking session, she demanded tantra. Ana, the manly one from Brazil, has tried to research it, but she is also confused. I understand that it is some kind of Hindu sex rite, but that's about all I can understand. I don't see how this could be a Hindu thing. Indians never struck me as being particularly sexual. If you told me it was Italian or Persian I might believe it.

Is tantra a skill of some kind? If so, how do I become proficient?

Thank you,

Mark Black

Dear Mark:

Thank you for your intelligent question! I love how you are thoughtfully curious and open-minded.

Tantra is such a broad subject, perhaps some more detailed questions would help me to ascertain more specifically what area is of most interest to you. However, I shall endeavor to respond to the questions you have here.

Tantra was in practice before the Hindu religion in various forms, but to our modern understanding has included some Hindu teachings as well. The ancient Tantric writings are said to have been scribed by men, but initially came from the Dakini's—enlightened, spiritual female teachers. Tantra is a spiritual path that is based on the ideals of consciousness, freedom, scientific tools, personal balance, pleasure & compassion. There are 64 arts in Tantra, and only one of them is sexuality—an area which needs a lot of healing in our culture right now.

On the Tantric path, we focus on optimizing our understanding of how to best activate and operate ourselves within this physical realm for expanding our consciousness, optimizing our experience, and the enjoyment of life.

In the sexual realm, we learn how to become more aware of ourselves as spirit within a body and energy in motion (Life Force or Orgasmic Energy). We learn how to open and activate our bodies and our hearts to expand our energy fields and raise our vibration to levels of higher consciousness, through pleasure. We learn how to manage this energy, use it, and share it. We consciously learn how to accept and integrate all of ourselves and bring our hearts and minds in total focus to share and expand our pleasure and connection. We learn how to create a strong foundation for heart-centered union in higher love that uplifts our perspective, centeredness, and stability. In learning these activation and attunement tools, the wonderful side effects include more love, intimacy, attunement, sexual skill, expanded and intensified orgasmic response, ejaculatory mastery, full body orgasms, more sensitivity and feeling, improved health and communication, and overall balance and well-being.

Some of the other Tantric arts are . . . Yoga, martial arts, flower arranging, dance, painting, food preparation, and more. The element that is common in all of these arts is focused attention, the use of breath, managed movement. These are the elements that bring your focus to the magical power of the NOW moment, so that the energy channeled through the body used in that moment is focused with a laser-like quality for maximum effect. Some call this a meditative approach.

Proficiency is attained through a strong passion for the arts, study and practice. It is preferable to begin with experiences with a qualified trainer/educator, for this is an art of the body and not the mind. You can try to learn from books, but the expectations that you may garner from reading may actually impede your practice, for it is important that you clue into your inner truth, experience, and response, rather than what the book may tell you. I do offer sessions for individuals and couples, and workshops in a group setting as well. The basic introductory practices are simple, very easy to learn, and bring amazing, immediate results. I hope this begins to answer some of your questions. Please feel free to discuss further.

Blessings,

Shiv

Dear Shiv,
Thank you for the intelligent and intelligible answer! I know what tantra is now, sort of. I am surprised that it is Indian, and not Italian or Persian. I have found their arts of love to be profound and thorough. The part I am completely confused about is complete body orgasms, as I've already conquered ejaculatory mastery.

I am thinking of bringing Ana, the masculine Brazilian, but as I think about it, I realize he/she may be an impediment. If I could have brought the Latvian who is very small, that would have been better. If I were to do individual sessions, how would they work, given the nature of this practice?
Regards,
Mark

Dear Mark,

A full body orgasm is where, instead of the orgasmic energy going down and out, you learn how to bring it up through the body activating every cell, so that they all are vibrating with energy and there is a rush through the central core of the body, like when you get turned on, that expands and extends upwards for however long you want to sustain it.

Blessings,

Shiv

D<small>ear</small> Shiv,

I already experience that with even the most simple of quickies and orgasms. But maybe I'm wrong. BTW, how would I know if every cell is being affected when I get that rush and vibration?

Thank you,

Mark

P.S. You have a gorgeous name.

Dear Mark:

Well, what I am explaining to you is what I am feeling in those types of orgasms. I certainly cannot scientifically "prove" that every cell is affected, but it does feel like it. There is an overall buzz/vibration that is felt everywhere, and this orgasm can be extended for as long as you choose to stay focused within the energy flow. The difference in this situation is that you can learn how generate this energy at will, without any stimulation needed, and the focus is not limited to the genital area and is diffused through the body.

Blessings,

Shiv

And this response, from another tantrist:

Dear Mark,

Thank you for your questions. Yes, Tantra is a vast subject. While Tantra is not a sexual technique, Tantra does have meditations that have to do with experiencing "that which cannot be named" in lovemaking. Where are you located? There are many wonderful books where you can begin to explore—there's one, it's in novel form but very accurate, called *Tantric Quest* by Daniel Odier.

I'm teaching an intro weekend in Santa Monica, January 15–16, you are most welcome to join us.

I've added you to the list to receive my weekly meditations and calendar updates, to give you some inspiration.

Much love,

Mary Johnson

D_{ear} Mary,

My extremely masculine lover in Latvia was wondering whether you plan on having an event there. She knows of many interested people in Riga. Perhaps we could do something on the television, or possibly as part of a convention? Apparently, once winter sets in, people become desperate for loving contact. It is a cold country with cold people, but I have found that a smile with holiness behind it breaks the ice. I know of a strange Turkish Sufi group/cult that went there last winter, and they loved it. I guess people there are very open to the divine. All those years of Stalin and Marx lying to them about the soul has caught up with them. Send me your thoughts. I am so curious!
Mark

Hi Mark,

I love that idea, please send my e-mail information to your Latvian lover. I agree, it's those types of cultures that can be so pure at the core. I also resonate with the cold people/cold weather and lots of sweetness just below the surface, there's something very warm about that—really authentic. Tantra goes so deep there.

Much love,

Mary

Dear Mary,

I love that you love that idea too. I agree that cold-weather people actually explode the most when tapped. This is my sixth long-term Latvian friend, and it has been the same with each one. This one in particular is very attached to me, I think mostly because she was neglected for so long, because she is so manly and (between us!) ugly in a conventional sense. She looks a lot like that overrated actor, Richard Gere, only a little hairier, but on a woman it just doesn't work. I don't know if she'd feel comfortable on television, to be honest. She has connections with people who have a cable channel, and I think they'd really be excited about learning about sexual tantra. They are from Afghanistan, and I think you'll find them lovely.

Look forward to hearing from you,

Mark

Hi Mark,

Sounds wonderful. Yes, please pass along my information to your Latvian friend, I look forward to hearing from her.

Very exciting!

Much love,

Mary

H i Mary,

We have been reading up on tantra together and are thinking that maybe it is best if we were to do this retreat and/or seminar at a nudist center in either Jamaica or Cairo. My lover spoke to some of her friends, and they feel that Latvians tend to be too lascivious. I know what she means. I had the same feeling when I was in Afghanistan with these contacts I told you about. It is always tricky getting the spiritual vibration and ambiance and general attitude toward enlightenment right, since there are so many losers and phonies in these circles who aren't there for the right reasons.

Thank you,

Mark

H̲i Mark,
Thanks for keeping me up to date. Enjoy the workshops in Jamaica or Cairo!
Much love,
Mary

Dear Organic Sex and Brandy Michener,

I found out about your upcoming event in Los Angeles and I am planning on attending. I have a question about your feelings on the ecological impact of my sexual life. It hasn't to do with biodegradable sex toys or organic high-thread-count bed sheets. It is that my lovers are spread out between Latvia, Saudi Arabia, Brazil, and Germany, but I live outside Santa Barbara. We are constantly flying around, trying to meet up. Soon we are having a party in Konigsberg, where all nine of us will finally be in the same place. This will be a low-impact raw-food event, which we may also replicate here in California, if it works out well the first time. One problem I have is that I am attracted to extremely short women, so it is difficult for me to be attracted to women in most nations.

I would love to hear your thoughts about what you think I can do. At least I can send you this paperless e-mail from my solar house! Regards,
Mark Black

Hi Mark,

Sorry to be so tardy with my response—have been extremely busy during the past few months. I apologize for not having an adequate answer to this question. You may want to carbon-offset your travel, but that's the advice I'd give to anyone whose work requires a lot of flying. With regard to your particular sexual peccadilloes, I haven't any advice.

By the way, I did not have any events in LA. You may be thinking of the Eco-Sex symposium that was put on by Annie Sprinkle in Santa Monica last month. I was not a part of that, although I was on the West Coast doing some events near San Francisco.

Cheers and good luck,

Brandy

Dear Aphrodite's Dungeons,
My son loves your dungeons, and he has asked to come there the day he turns eighteen. I was wondering if we could rent an area for he and his friends (about ten total), as well as me and my lover from Saudi Arabia. We are all of normal height, except that my lover is unusually short. I hope you will be able to accommodate her as well.

I would like to have a birthday cake delivered, with one of your women inside of it. I believe it is the ultimate gift for a young man. We are thinking to come in after breakfast, rather than late at night. Maybe it is cheaper then?

I admire that you make every effort to keep the place clean.

My son has a foot fetish (we are very open sexually), which is the main thing I hope you can satisfy. I believe my lover and I would want to experience the wrestling, meanwhile.

The cages and the Chinese palace look amazing!
Thank you,
Mark Black
Montecito, California

Dear Mark,
That's one fantasy that even I never heard of . . . it would be amazing . . .
but not cheap . . . when were you thinking and make sure every one
is over 18 . . . that cake, if you want a real one, would be expensive as
well.
Aphrodite's

CHAPTER SEVEN
MARK'S SPIRITUAL NEEDS

D_{ear} Tracy Weston,

I found you when I did a search for a life coach, and I really like your approach. My situation in life has become complicated. I have a house here and a tiny one in Konigsberg, Germany, and then I have a luxury consultancy business in Saudi Arabia. I have a half-Indian lover from Saudi Arabia who is very short, and then a very tall lover from Latvia, whom I am supposed to meet in Mallorca in a few weeks.

I reveal the details because it is important for you to know that I am having issues with women overseas, always at a distance. Most of this is due to the fact that I am obsessed with finding women of extreme heights, and they are usually not found here.

I feel like I am missing something in myself. No matter how much money I spend on my home, or what car I buy for my girlfriends, I end up feeling empty. I don't want simple answers or new-age formulas. I met the Dalai Lama, and that was totally stupid. They said that would change my life inevitably. Not. I've never had a life coach. I've been a fierce individualist, a Daniel Boone who flies more than he wants to. I'm curious to know what magic you can work.

Thank you,

Mark Black

Montecito, California

Dear Mark,

Your situation is not uncommon. Somewhere along the way you were taught that you needed to accomplish particular things in order to have value. And that certain "undesirable" acts or preferences somehow diminished that value. Of course, success does not prevent one from realizing his true value, but it does make it more difficult to fully access and to enjoy.

Your preferences in women and how far from you they may be are not a problem in the way that you might believe. The emptiness that you feel and the distance that you create are symptoms of a much broader, yet very solvable issue. I have found that a person's level of success in life often compromises their ability to shift the inner workings which must adjust in order for them to feel truly fulfilled. But when individuals have allowed me to guide them on challenging and tumultuous journeys inward, they are able to achieve true and lasting joy, peace, and satisfaction. They begin to feel and appreciate more than they ever believed was possible. The same power that made you successful can also make you extremely, genuinely happy, if you are truly ready and open to that path. I honor you for reaching out to me, for knowing that you need a guide at this point in your life. But before I will take a phone consultation with you, I want you to really think about what you're asking for. Are you really ready to rip your self-judgment wide open and release it? Are you willing to do the extensive work necessary to conquer your fears of rejection and failure in order to finally live a life of true, rich, deep, lasting bliss? If I take you as a client, I already know that you will be a royal pain in my ass. People like you aren't accustomed to being told what to do, not even by someone who knows exactly what they need. But I love what I do, and I love the challenge of turning someone who is his own worst enemy into someone who loves his life and appreciates himself and his life's work more than he ever thought possible. Picture yourself looking out at the sunset with your ideal partner, weeping with gratitude because of the overwhelming sensation of having never felt a previous moment so perfectly and so fully as the one you are experiencing. Please think carefully about whether you are truly prepared to embark on the adventure of your life. Do you have the space to bring up your demons right now? Is your schedule flexible enough for the dramatic shifts that will occur? This work is extremely powerful, and some days you won't even be able to get out of bed. Some days you will need to allow yourself the space to do whatever feels right, instead of what you "need to do." Can you deal with that right now? Please take some time. Let me know if and when you believe you are ready.

Sincerely,

Tracy Weston

Life Coach ~ Energy Worker

Dear Sedona Crystal and Gem Emporium,
Flying in next month and I was wondering about two things. What is
the largest Buddha you have and which crystal do you carry that you
believe is the most powerful for someone who is a hedonist? To make
your best suggestion you'll probably want to know where I am in life. I
am a happy person, but I've had to spend a lot of time in Saudi Arabia
lately, and my business is a disaster. To make up for that, I read a lot of
books about getting enlightened (usually the Dalai Lama or essays by
this one German guy I met in Bali). I am addicted to the women in my
life, and I can't break away. I have been to addiction clinics, and they
help, but eventually I end up reattached. I need to meditate more. My
friends tell me that coming to Sedona will get me focused again, that
a good crystal will speed things up. I am after purification of my soul.
I'd like to know if you agree with their assessment, and whether you
think you can be of assistance.
Thank you,
Mark Black

H i Mark,

Thank you for your interest in our store. The best thing is for you is to come in when you are in town. With crystals, we usually feel drawn to the ones that can be most helpful at the moment, so it is a very individual thing. I could suggest different things, but again, the best is if you can experience and have time to see what's there. We also offer Psychic Readings, Chakra Balancing Sessions, and energy and body work, and I could imagine some of the treatments we do, like the Psychic Energy Massage, could be good for you.

Let me know if you have any more questions.

Abhichandra

Sedona Crystals

Dear Sri Sri Babaji Glazer,
I would like to speak directly to God, especially the God inside myself,
the one we breathe in and out, but mostly in. I came across your
Website, and I believe that you could show me the way, because I
believe with all my mind body that it is about what we eat.

I have suffered greatly in my life, mostly because I have been
abandoned by too many lovers. I have a tendency to choose abusive
women who take advantage of me because I am a softy at heart. I am
a happy, peaceful man. I have two houses with raw kitchens. But I am
missing God. One of those women kept trying to get me to cook my
food and practically force-fed me, no matter how much I told her I
needed to stay raw.

Can you help me find God, or a feeling of holiness? I don't really
like to meditate, and I have an aversion to tantra and mandalas, but
everything else is really cool to me. Oh, and I won't do yoga. Pilates
works, but also any form of experience that is soul-based. No mention
of the Dalai Lama, please. I only care about being spiritual. I want to
be a shrine to divinity and boundless radiant love.
Thank you,
Mark Black
Montecito, California

Dear Mark,

Aloha from Hawaii, and Namaste,

What you have shared here is noble, i.e., that you are eating purely, and especially that you want to be a shrine of divinity and shine light on all. The two are connected. Just be sure that your eating regimen is not a form of food-faddism, but rather that you are eating consciously and taking the energy from pure food "up the spine" by mingling it with conscious thinking, selfless acting, and focused meditation; then all will be well. It is a Kundalini technique, actually, which is partly a tantric path . . . like it or not. In other words, pure food gives pure blood. Pure blood gives pure thoughts. Pure thoughts give pure mind, and pure mind is God.

To talk to God one does not need to move the lips. In fact, God is essentially formless, i.e., has no ears . . . or hears through all ears, depending how one thinks of it. Meditation, if done properly, is a form of communicating with God. The more silent the mind becomes, the closer one will be in proximity to the inner Self, Atman—what you call here the "God inside myself."

Disappointment in people, in personalities, is common to all here on this earth. Just forgive them and be content with lonely study. A sense of holiness will dawn over time, if the mind is focused on the Source of Existence, rather than the mere effects of it . . . i.e., the worlds of name and form.

If you want to exchange e-mails, I am here and do it every day with many students and others who write in. Sending all support for your noble endeavors,

Peace x 3,

Babaji

Dear Sri Sri Babaji,
Strange. I just left Maui yesterday!

As for your letter, the truth of the matter is that I am a despicable person. All I think about is seducing extremely short women from other countries, and having plenty of money. At first I was afraid to make this confession, but now that you've asked me to ask you, I feel I must open up. At one point I became a Sufi, just because there were easy women there. I didn't like those people one bit. Then I did the same with Tibetan Buddhism (where the women were even easier, but also very angry), and even one Christian group in Tennessee. I lived in India so that I could seduce these naïve mystical types. That's why I say that I'm complicated and impure. I've made a lot of money, but at other people's expense. I need for whoever it is that gets me on the right path to know what it means to be obsessed by short women, or something like that.

Do you feel like you're holy?
Thank you again,
Mark

Dear Mark,
Aloha and Namaste.

To address your main admittance first, I must say "mahalo" for being honest and straightforward. It seems by what you are telling me that sexuality and the passion of lust are at the root of your disorientation, or lack of the sacred in your life and mind. Do you also feel a sense of women being holy, or are they just sex objects? If you feel the divine in them, even a little, then it might be a good starting point to look upon them as the Divine in human form. Of course, it would help if you found a certain one who was both worthy of your worship/love and who saw the same potential in you—what is called a consecrated partner, or wife, or life partner. Practicing mutual love together, all the less worthy things in the mind get taken up and transformed in such an atmosphere. I do not know you well, so I am only offering advice here that I have seen others take into consideration and benefit by.

As for your second question, one cannot, should not, say such things about oneself. I can say, however, that I have met truly holy people—a few—in my life, and meditate upon others I have come to know are holy, which is a very great blessing. Now I strive to exemplify them.

May God help us both to realize our cherished ideals.
Peace x 3,
Babaji

Dear Tibetan Master Rinpoche,

I have done everything a man can do in his life, and I believe most of my lifetimes. I have a pile of money and lovers and material possessions and spiritual books. I only read spiritual books. The rest I consider to be dirty and I won't touch them. My life is about purity and sanctity and eating.

The problem I have is that I am having trouble with my meditations, because all I think about when I sit down with the prayers I learned in Dharamsala and that silly town of Woodstock, New York is linguini puttanesca. I can't explain my fascination with this Italian specialty.

It is my downfall. I have spoken to people about it, and they tell me that it will pass. I promise you I don't think about the gorgeous women in my life or all my problems with incompetent employees. I smell puttanesca when I'm meditating. Of course there is nowhere for me to find a solution to this in the teachings, so I ask you for your counsel.

I had the same problem when I was a Sufi, but thank God I got out of that, even though I liked the food, especially what they did with chickpeas there after Ramadan. They were also great with eggplant.

I am sure you have your hands full with all the problems of your students and their endless questions, but I hope you have a moment for me.

Thank you,

Mark Black

Montecito, California

P.S. I hope you come and teach here one day! This city is full of people on the path to enlightenment.

Dear Mark,

Your question brings up a number of questions related to the main point of meditation and how to bring all of the variety of life's experiences onto the path. You might want to take a look at Rinpoche's Silence and Happiness of Living, or take part in a Celebration of Living weekend.

In general, Rinpoche emphasizes that all experiences can be brought into one's meditation practice by simply bringing mind to the experience. The practice has less to do with 'purity and sanctity,' and more to do with how we tame our wild 'Monkey mind,' in such a way that allows us to recognize the abiding wisdom and goodness that is our basic nature.

Good luck along the way.

Sincerely,

Kevin Martin, Tenzin International

D_ear Esalen Institute,
I am considering making a personal retreat with my Saudi Arabian friend whom I want to make my girlfriend, but that's a long story. I was there about two years ago as we drove up the coast, and I was so disappointed that you were already fully booked with some kind of conference.

In order to be able to stay there, I need to know a few things. First of all, I would like to know if you use organic towels and bed sheets (the thread count?), and what kind of water filtration you use. I have sensitive skin and allergies that require particular care. I provide my own bath products as a result. I need to know if the rooms are silent and if you happen to know at what decibel level the quiet is. I am a sensitive sleeper, and non-natural noises make it impossible for me to sleep. The same goes for the issue of whether the room can be fully darkened. Have there ever been any bedbug reports in your rooms? I am afraid of all bugs, but especially all bedbugs, given a terrible attack I experienced when I was on retreat in northern India. I would like to know what your policy is regarding picking our own food from your garden. My friend is something of a habitual fruit thief (she goes around my neighborhood stealing citrus off people's trees), so I need to forewarn her about what you expect from her.

I am a Kantian, so if there is any reason you would like me to lecture on the philosopher I would be glad to do so. I have noticed that people in hot tubs like to talk philosophy, so perhaps I will do most of my public speaking there in your hot-spring pools.

I would like to make sure that I am housed as far as possible from incense and anyone doing yoga. It is my great worry with spending a week at your place, because I find yoga to be objectionable.

Given how harmonious a place Esalen is supposed to be, I think you will understand my concerns.
Thank you,
Mark Black
Montecito, California

Hello Mark Black,

I'll do my best to answer your questions, though it sounds from your requirements, Esalen may not be a "good fit" for you to visit.

We don't use organic sheets or towels. I don't know the thread count, though you may contact our Cabins department at (831) 667-3019 to check.

Regarding noise, some of our rooms are quieter than others. Our premium rooms and Point Houses have additional sound proofing. Be aware Esalen can be a noisy place at times, as some leaders may encourage students to "whoop it up" as part of releasing stuck energy. We also have regular ceremonies and celebrations, which may involve drumming and music.

We haven't had reports of bed bugs.

As far as harvesting from our gardens, you would need permission of the Garden manager.

If you wish to pursue teaching or lecturing here, you'll need to contact our programs department. See below for more information.

You should be aware that there are numerous yogis here, and we offer regular yoga workshops and daily yoga classes on our Movement program.

Best wishes,

The Esalen Office

Forty minutes later the following arrived:

Hi Mark,

Thanks for your interest in Esalen. After reading your requirements we feel that you would not be comfortable staying here. There is yoga practiced here at many locations and its philosophy is respected here. Also incense is sometimes used. Thanks for your inquiry, and we hope that you can enjoy a retreat at an organization more in line with your needs and philosophies.

Best Regards,
Esalen Office

Disappointed, but never one to give up, I decided to try somewhere similar on the East Coast, the Omega Institute. The following was their reply:

G̲ood Day Mark,

Thank you for your interest in Omega Institute. Answers to your questions are below. In our ADDX (Green rooms) we have organic beds, pillows, and comforters. Not all sheets and none of the towels are organic. We are located in the country and there are quite often nature sounds such as geese, woodpeckers, etc. The cabins were all built over a period of many years, and some are more quiet than others, however even in a quiet one it's possible to hear your neighbor open and close their door. Some of the doors are quite loud. The rooms are not fully darkened. We do have low-level ambient lighting around campus. We do not currently have bedbugs. If someone does report them, we look into it right away. So far, the searches have turned up negative. Keep in mind that we are in the country, and there are bugs around, including spiders and ticks. We cannot prevent them from being in rooms. Our vegetable garden is used for the cafe only, and guests are not allowed to pick anything. Thank you for your offer of lecturing, but our schedule is always quite full. Just so you know, we do not have a hot spring. Just a lake. While Omega is not a yoga center, we do offer daily open yoga, meditation, movement, and tai chi classes. Many of our participants have a yoga practice as well and may do some outdoors. We cannot guarantee you would not be near someone doing yoga. As for incense, we do not permit candles or incense in the cabins, but the bookstore does sell incense, so it's possible you will smell it if you browse in there.

Please don't hesitate to e-mail or call me if there is anything else I may help with.

Kind Regards,

Omega Registration

CHAPTER EIGHT
MARK'S LITERARY NEEDS

Dear Nobel Prize Committee,

Over the years I have had many dreams about winning the Nobel Prize for Literature. Unfortunately, I don't have the literary success and readership I also dreamt for myself.

My girlfriend from Saudi Arabia is my voice of reason who reminds me that I'm a total failure. She loves me nevertheless, for some reason. Maybe it is because I chased her for twenty-two years, with well over fifty visits to Riyadh, before I made her mine, despite her father's protests.

I gave him signed copies of my self-published essays, but he still didn't accept my overtures towards his daughter.

This all serves as an introduction to my comedic, but tragic, essay about chasing this girl for over two decades and facing nothing but rejection. It mirrors my professional life as a writer. It is one of the most pathetic stories you've ever heard, in all honesty. But I was committed to something higher in my life than going down to a pub and picking up any old person.

I am hoping I can submit my autobiographical story for consideration for the Nobel Prize for Literature. I can self-publish it, if that would help my chances.

My friend Hamid Hamid, a chef in Santa Barbara, is making a documentary to go along with the essay. It is called *One Hundred Thousand Nights of Agony as I Flew to Saudi Arabia in Search of Her.*

Thank you,

Mark Black

Montecito, California

Dear Mr. Black,

Thank you for your e-mail. No person can nominate herself/himself. Qualifications to nominate candidates vary somewhat among the Nobel Prize-Awarding Institutions. If you have any further questions about the nomination process, please contact the prize awarding institutions.

Yours sincerely,

Nobel Media Team

D̲ear Grammar Lady,

I have a question that I hope you can answer, so I wonder if you would mind doing that? When I write, I feel obliged to transform most sentences into the interrogative form, and that makes me feel crazy because, as you can imagine (can't you?), it would become agonizing. At my place of work they are used to it, but when I write customers, I sense their ambivalence and my numbers drop. Have you heard of this disorder before? I thought if anybody would, you would, so do I need to stand corrected?

Mark Black

Montecito, California

Mark,

I have a bad feeling that I didn't answer this question yet. Sometimes when the messages come to school, I don't see them, or they become part of the huge pileup I have here! Sorry about that!

You asked about writing things as questions rather than statements. This is kind of a deferral to other people. You are giving them your power by doing so.

I'm glad that you recognize that it isn't helping you. Try to restate them in positive statements; this will make you seem less unsure of yourself without coming on as aggressive.

Grammar Lady

Dear Professor Heiler,

All my life I ignored the study of philosophy, focusing instead on taxidermy. That is because my mother used to read Nietzsche to me as a young boy every night as I went to sleep. We went through all the aphorisms from beginning to end, starting from before I went to school. She wanted me to be an Overman. I decided to study taxidermy after high school because I wanted, I later realized, to do a reevaluation of all values. Staying with those aphorisms and all I learned wasn't going to cut it. My mother wouldn't talk to me for ten years. Things change. She died, but in the end she told me that I am an Overman nevertheless.

I would like to know what you suggest as a remedy for my predicament. I don't know what I am, but her words in her dying days haunt me still.

Mark Black

Dear Mark,

I myself think that the idea of the Overman is a metaphor for every person's potential to leave behind social expectations and devise a way of life for her or himself. So everyone has an Overman inside, but nobody literally is an Overman.

Best,

HR

Dear Literary Agent Helen Martin-Feiner,
I am looking for representation on my memoir, *Under the Castle Lives a Gentleman*, about a gentleman, myself, who lives in a tiny house (that his mother bought him), which lies underneath a castle in Konigsberg, the town that produced Immanuel Kant, a philosopher he despises.

This gentleman consumes himself with certain passions, including keeping a lifelong set of very short women as lovers, stealing cases of Latour wine from various wine dealers, and hosting events of snake, rock, paper, scissors matches for the German League.

The very short women lovers that I keep have written me six cartons full of love letters, including photographs that correspond to the history of Germany over the last twenty-five years. I have written nothing about them, meanwhile. But that is only part of the story.

My best friend, in Montecito, suggested I move into her pavilion about ten years ago because she was missing my company. That led to the formation of a luxury consultant business, which forces me to spend more time than I like to in Saudi Arabia.

I maintain there a group of women that I must keep anonymous, because they are also married. I have letters written in Arabic and English from these women as well, which I imagine would fill the middle of the book, because, unlike most memoirs, this will be about what others say about me. I'm not interested in talking about myself. That is so boring. The pavilion burned down in the last set of fires over here, but I was able to save the letters. I ended up sleeping in my friend's bedroom, because she has had psychological issues since the fire. I have asked her to write about me as a child, so that would be a chunk of the story too.

I have all kinds of ideas about how people should be living instead of how they are living. For example, I am working on contacting our Governor about educating drivers in California to use cruise control more often. I believe it will save lives and reduce our energy dependence far more than most measures. I believe fashion models ought to be shorter and more realistic and am planning on using money from my book to start a charity for body dysmorphism issues. Last, I believe that poetry can solve most of the problems in the world. I hope to litter the book with poetry that demonstrates the path for human beings.

I will forward you chapters and letters with your permission. Please let me know if you are interested in representing my book.

Sincerely,

Mark Black

D_{ear} Mark,

Thanks for your query. Mind sending along the first five pages of your manuscript in the body of an e-mail? I'd be happy to take a look and let you know whether the style is the best fit for me.

Thanks,

Helen Martin-Feiner

Dear Professor Hartry Field,
As a city organizer for Shrewsbury, MO, it is my honor to invite you, a renowned mathematician, to speak at the festivities for the renaming of Hartry Park. You may have even heard about it. We have decided to name it Hartry Field, as part of an overall revival attempt by the city. It is a special town, with one of the nicest aquatic facilities in the state. Would you be willing to address our town during the ceremony? It would be an honor to have you.
Thank you,
Mark Black

D ear Mark,

I'm very pleased to hear about the renaming of Hartry Park. It will help me in the competition with my daughter, Elizabeth Wrigley-Field (her mother's last name is Wrigley). She takes great pride in the fact that an obscure baseball stadium is "named after her." I'll be on the lookout for news that the Cardinals will be moving their facilities to your newly renamed park.

Best wishes,

Hartry Field

CHAPTER NINE
MARK'S SCHOOLING NEEDS

Dear Exorcism Training,

I have a potential girlfriend from Latvia who would like to become an exorcist if she comes here to live with me in California. That is the one condition she gave me, after I stayed up all night pleading with her that I needed her. I am a little confused about why she is so focused on learning to be an exorcist, but she's so kind usually (it depends on the time of the month, though) that I am worried slightly about my safety. She tells me that it is for the good of humanity that she wants to do this, but I saw that famously terrifying movie, and I'm afraid she will become like that. Though she is very short, she is powerful. I think she has a high IQ, based on some testing I did on her the other day. She's a spiritual powerhouse. I know that because I have been to see high rabbis in Jerusalem, and she is a little like them. That's why I am so madly in love with her. I don't know why she doesn't feel the same way about me, but I'm hoping that with some training in exorcism, she will begin to worship me a little bit too.

Is it true that exorcism will make her more loving?

Thank you. I look forward to your response.

Mark Black

Greetings, Mark,

Becoming an exorcist won't make her love you more or less. If she wants to learn how to do exorcism, the first thing she must learn is to be soft and honest with herself. Don't be afraid, exorcisms in movies and stuff like that have nothing to do with the real thing, it's just less dramatic than we think and more powerful than we could imagine. I suggest her to be guided and don't try her first exorcism alone, because when we do that we stay with the influence of any demons or succubes that could be in the body or in the house, and we are not experienced enough to see the difference in our attitude.

The most powerful exorcism is not done with power, but with kindness and true love, and it's the difficult part to get.

If you have any problems or questions, don't hesitate.

Vashista

Assistant of MahaBhakti

Dear Vashista,

That's crazy. I am obsessed by succubes. Does that mean that they're in the house? In the body? I asked my lover, and she won't tell me what's happening, but I can tell that her soul understands something that I don't. Something tells me that she'll be a phenomenal exorcist. Thank you!

Mark

P.S. BTW, what kind of name is Vashista? It is beautiful.

Dear Mark,

Can I ask you what makes you think that you have succubes? Did you feel something wrong with you in your body or in your mind?

PS: Vashista is a sage who helped Goddess Indra.

H<small>i, Vashista,</small>

Nothing is wrong, but these succubes keep showing up in my dreams. They are ferocious, sexually.

BTW, based on your experiences, do you think I should use a name for spirituality?

Thank you,

Mark

Hi, Mark,

Okay, if doesn't bother you too much that's fine. But you could take care of it by yourself.

It's a good idea to use a name for our spirituality. Generally we use Sanskrit or Hebrew, because both of these languages are sacred and used for spirituality. Try to find something that means something for you, and if you are not sure, I can help you.

Vashista is my soul name, given by my spiritual master, MahaBhakti, but if don't know yours, you can use something else until you have a revelation.

Vashista

D<small>ear</small> Vashista,
I wonder, based on your intuition and what you know about me, what you would rename me?

I am dying of curiosity!
Mark (only Mark)

Dear Vashista,
Tell me what you feel about Mark Black's pure soul concept, and I'll find the Sanskrit name for it.
Thank you,
Maha

Dear Mark,
Do you have a photo of you, so we can focus on you?
Thank you,
Maha

Maha and Vashista,

Attached is a photo. I like Sanskrit and Hebrew, but I really prefer Aramaic and Swedish, as I have done a lot of meditation in the Lapland.

You don't know how much I appreciate this.

Mark

D_{ear} Vashista,

Pretty good. The earth element, the generator, has something to do with righteousness, as it does what should be. The Sanskrit term is Bhavya, the auspicious and fortunate, what should be, or what would be the best possibility, and it does influence the other term: Kara, the action.

Bhavyakar = thriving to be righteous, virtuous, to do the right thing, to inspire right-action, responsibility, and has a gracious and pleasant aspect sub-implied in the name. Bhavya also means pleasant, gracious, handsome, depending on the context, because it means "good outcome," both in action, feeling, while it is happening, and in the final result. It's not obvious to give an English translation of a word so wide in interpretations.

Maha

Dear Boston University Dental Admissions,
I am a tooth specialist who practices as a semi-taxidermal analyst for the German government, here in Konigsberg, where I live with my young wife and four German shepherds. My family are all dental specialists who have the full training that is available at a school by the local castle. I am competitive by nature, an alpha male, so my dream is to come to the USA and enlist at your university, the finest, best one in the world for such study, according to the latest German study.

I have two questions: The first is whether you accept married Germans, and the second is whether you know if dogs are allowed in your student housing quarters on campus in Philadelphia, Pennsylvania, USA.

Thank you,
Mark Black

Dear Mark,

Thank you for your interest in Boston University Henry M. Goldman School of Dental Medicine. We require applicants to the DMD program to have or be completing a Bachelors Degree from the United States or Canada. Internationally trained dentists are eligible to apply for the Advanced Standing, two-year program or any Post-Doctoral Programs. We do accept married students. For more information please review our Website, and any questions can be submitted via the following e-mails for the programs:

> Advanced Standing: <u>asdent@bu.edu</u>
> Post-Doctoral: <u>postadm@bu.edu</u>

For information regarding housing and whether dogs are allowed, please contact the Office of Housing, at housing@bu.edu. Please do not hesitate to contact us with any further information or questions.
Best,
Boston University Henry M. Goldman School of Dental Medicine

CHAPTER TEN
MARK'S SAUDI LOVER'S NEEDS

Dear San Ysidro Ranch,

On my way back to California after living for sixteen years in Dubai and Saudi Arabia, I am interested in staying at the magnificent Warner Cottage in October, for I think it would be the ideal way to repatriate. I will be landing at the Santa Barbara airport, and I travel with my own mattress and the complete works of Martin Heidegger.

First I will be going to dinner at a midget friend's in Montecito. I could have my Brazilian female assistants bring the mattress to the master bedroom of the cottage, if that would be permissible to you. Setup of the Swedish mattress never takes more than half an hour. I wouldn't be requiring the changing of the mattresses in any of the other rooms. My friends aren't as picky as I.

Looking forward to hearing from you,

Mark Black

Dear Mr. Black,

I would be happy to reserve the Warner Cottage for you. On what evenings would you like to relax with us? We will need a credit card to reserve the room, and with our Warner and Kennedy Premier accommodations, we require one night's deposit, nonrefundable. We look forward to your visit. The mattress will not be an issue. We will need the names of your associates who will have access to your room prior to your arrival, to allow them entry.

Please let me know if I may be of further assistance.

Kind regards,

Guest Services, San Ysidro Ranch

900 San Ysidro Lane

Santa Barbara, CA 93108

Dear Brink's Armored Truck Delivery,
I have a girlfriend who is arriving at LAX next week. She is from
Saudi Arabia, and she is rather paranoid about coming to the USA.
She's heard all kinds of horror stories about the crime situation here.
I've tried convincing her that it is really not as dire a situation as she
imagines.

I have to make her feel comfortable, if I wish to keep her, so I am
wondering whether you're able to assist me with transporting her to
my home near Santa Barbara. Tell me if you have seating in the back
of your trucks, or if seating can be temporarily installed. While I care
about her comfort, I think guaranteeing her safety will put her mind
at rest once and for all.
I look forward to hearing from you,
Mark Black

Dear Mr. Black,
Unfortunately we do not provide individual transportation services
and will not be able to assist with your request.

Thank you, and have a nice day.
Brink's

Dear Security Professionals of North America,
Today I am writing you about securing the services of approximately four armed bodyguards for my lover, who will be visiting me from Saudi Arabia. She is an unusually short woman and highly passionate nevertheless. Appropriate bodyguards for a person of this temperament and size are a must. Over a period of two weeks we will be going between my homes in Germany and Montecito, California, as well as a quick stop in Azerbaijan to meet with my ex-wife. I imagine needing only two guards for the portion of travel overseas. The main area of concern is my home in Montecito, a private, gated property, during the late hours. That would be for October 18 through October 24. I have received no threats, but I am deeply concerned about guaranteeing my lover's safety during those days and will go to great lengths to protect her.

I have an armored vehicle, so that isn't an issue.
Thank you,
Mark Black

Mark,

Send me the locations pls.

    We can offer anywhere in the USA and internationally.

Albert Ramos

Dear Huntington Beach Aston Martin,

I am picking up my girlfriend from Saudi Arabia next week at LAX. She is less than five feet tall (all my lovers are), and my thought is to purchase a vehicle for her. I would probably want to buy a pre-owned vehicle, but make it look as if it were new.

Her English is not very good, but please don't speak French or Arabic with her. Can we arrange for a test drive of the cheapest vehicle on your floor that looks good?

I would like to fill the car with roses before we go. I can handle that part.

Thank you,

Mark Black

Montecito, California

M<small>ark,</small>

Which car were you looking at to purchase? I have a few Vantage Coupe's in stock (manual transmission), which are our lowest priced vehicles. Also, was it Wednesday this week you wanted to come by?

Please advise.

Thanks,

Jose Ramirez

Dear Total Chic Personal Shoppers,
In the coming weeks my extremely short, but volatile, lover from Saudi Arabia and my extremely tall, but calm, lover from Latvia will be visiting me, and we plan on going shopping together. The issue is their heights; one is 4'8", and the other is 6'3", but both are 140 lbs. I hope they can go to the same stores. Yes, I want a shopping day, and the budget is approximately $100,000.00.

I've been overwhelmed with details planning out our vacation time together, including wine tours and hot air balloon afternoons, as well as a huge party. I need to go to Mallorca in the interim to attend a Borges seminar, so I won't have time to figure out where to take them.

That's when I found your service! I would love it if you could handle everything. They are extremely spoiled women, so nothing but the best will do. They are into leather products. That said, I am something of a miser, so I would like to find suitable stores that would make them believe I am spending more money than I am. Is the issue of their respective heights going to present a problem?

I look forward to hearing from you.
Mark Black
Montecito, California

Hi Mark-

Thank you for contacting TotalChic. I work with many Middle Eastern women, but am a bit unclear as to what you need.

I will send you our service agreement, which requires a credit card to hold the booking. You can pay with credit card, check, or cash the day of the shopping experience.

Will they be able to fill out our questionnaire online or should I ask you the information we need?

Best regards,

Stephanie Doyle

Dear Washington Caviar Corporation,
I am thinking to purchase a great deal of caviar for a party I am going to throw to celebrate the reuniting with an old lover I met in Saudi Arabia on November 18.

What do you do when you meet the love of your life again after many years? That is my situation. I am happy!

What is the maximum amount of Ossetra I can purchase?

We will be having about 2000 people over at the house, so I figure I would need about a half pound to full pound per person. It would be my gift to each person who attends. Please let me know about pricing and availability and quality of this product at this point in time.
Thank you,
Mark Black
Montecito, California

Dear Mark,

Your "situation" sounds wonderful. Congratulations, a dream come true.

Washington Caviar would love to be a part of the celebration. We can certainly supply the needed caviar. Washington Caviar has sustainable caviar that is priced from $65 per ounce to $125 per ounce. The best and most consistent quality, in my opinion, is the White sturgeon that is native to the West Coast of the US. This caviar has a large bead, wonderful colour, and most importantly, a marvelous flavor profile. The caviar we supply will be fresh, new-catch, 2010 production.

Washington Caviar can deliver for your party on November 18, 2010, number-one-quality White Sturgeon caviar; (all of our caviar is sustainable and legally harvested).

(1) 2,000 x 2oz per jar (250 lbs caviar) at $170 per jar = $340,000 US

(2) 2,000 x 4oz per tin (500 lbs caviar) at $340 per tin = $680,000 US

(3) 2,000 x 8oz per tin (1,000 lbs caviar) at $680 per tin = $1,360,000 US

(4) 2,000 X 1 lbs per tin (2,000 lbs caviar) at $1,360 per tin = $2,720,000 US

Washington Caviar puts all caviar orders in a black insulated gift bag. Please look at our Website to see the bag. If you would like to present your gift in an insulated bag, may we propose that custom insulated bags be fabricated for the gift. The bags take six weeks to produce in the US factory and are of very nice quality. We would need your camera-ready art for the printing on the bags. A great presentation and keepsake. Just a thought. Cost is $4.28 per piece.

If you would like quotes on different quantities and pack styles, please let us know. Washington Caviar will need to stage all packaging and proper crew to pack the order. It would be best to ship via refrigerated truck, and that will take a few days to deliver.

Barry Kingsman

Washington Caviar

Dear Jimmy Orin Photography,

I came across your Universal Portraits series last year and, impressed by the quality of the work, handed it to one of my assistants to file for future use when I would need a photographer.

The reason I am contacting you today is that in one month I am having a big party at my home, because I am coming together with my lover after chasing her for twenty-two years. She seems to have agreed to join me for the rest of my life. It is a very long story, this love story, and I have recorded much of it on video. Required to get this love of my life were countless visits to her home in Riyadh. She almost killed me with "no's." Now I am a much older, wealthier man, but I missed out on so much time with her. What's left I want to be with her, so I promised her a party like no other party. I bought her an almost-new Jaguar. I promised her that none of my other lovers and none of my ex-lovers would be present. That will prove difficult, but I will oblige.

I'm sorry to speak at length, but I wish to impress upon you the drama of the event for me. There will be rare animals present. I can barely contain myself when I write about it. Yes, I am an emotional man, to a fault. My years as a consultant after law school were trying ones.

It would be my honor if you would agree to document the event for us in the unique way I believe you can. I want the whole story laid out in stills. I promise you that nothing pornographic will take place, so you needn't worry. The other lovers will not be notified about the event, and I have my fingers crossed that they will not find out through the grapevine. There will be a lot of music and emotion.

I hope to invite approximately 1800 people, but most of those live far away, and so it is more of a formality. As far as where you come in, I believe it will be a threefold mission. Some flexibility on your part is necessary, but I will compensate you accordingly. My hope is that you would capture it in photographs, and I plan to hire someone to handle the video element, with several cameras. I would like you to record my first meeting with Fatimah in the baggage claim area at the Santa

Barbara airport. I know someone at the airport who has agreed to set up an area in the back as a temporary studio.

When we go outside, I plan on giving her the Jaguar. I need to record that moment. Then one video cameraman and you will accompany her and me to the house in the Jaguar.

Once we reach the country road, we will take a horse and wagon to the house, where our guests will already be waiting. I would like portraits of each guest, plus a record of the party.

There will be a lot going on at the party. I am inviting a circus troupe from Philadelphia and a small symphony. That's just part of it. I don't want to say too much, because I want the feeling of surprise to come through in your work. It may be a lot to document, so I don't mind if you don't capture every moment of it. I'm not Japanese, after all.

I want an impressionistic and artistic record of the lengths I am going to for this woman. She still hasn't agreed to be with me, but I believe this may finally rectify that.

The final phase of documenting will be following us up to our bedroom. I don't want anything beyond that, as I am not into anything pornographic. If you can hang around and document the morning breakfast, that would be great, too.

I hope this is a helpful explanation. It is rather straightforward, really. I'd love to hear your thoughts, as I am not sharing it with the people in my circle. They can't keep their traps shut!

I look forward to hearing your thoughts,

Mark Black

Montecito, California (but in London right now)

Greetings Mark,

Thank you for your kinds words in regards to my photography.

This is most certainly an intriguing request. I would love to know what work on the site most interests you. 22 years in the making. This all sounds like it will make for a very intense and amazing time. Drama, emotion, celebration, and a question mark or two. I am very interested. It reminds me a bit of a project I worked on for the artist Christo. I am at my creative best when I am given a situation and can create within it. It sounds like this is what you want to happen.

The only caveat I would throw in is that it may be difficult to photograph both the event itself and to photograph all the guests. My suggestion would be to set up an area where guests can be photographed with the lighting and background all ready to go. I'm guessing that perhaps there may be guests who prefer not to be photographed? If so, this gives them the option, and they will not feel forced.

The set-up can be as simple or as creative as you wish, as far as the background used. Also, you could get more creative and create a kind of artistic photo booth that the guests enter to take their own photos. Just a thought. I live in the Los Angeles (though please do not mistake me for a Paparazzi, never have, never will) area, and perhaps we could meet upon your return from London?

Cheers,

Jimmy Orin

CHAPTER ELEVEN
MARK'S RESIDENTIAL NEEDS

Dear Hansen Pools and Jacuzzis of Santa Barbara,
I am considering adding an Olympic swimming pool near the pavilion on my property. This is a private matter, and you will understand why. I have a harem that I am starting for myself, gathering for the first time the short women lovers I have in both Latvia and Brazil. I would need to know that you are willing to do this work in complete privacy.

There will be many women on the property while the work is going on, and I need your full cooperation if we are to work together. These are not paid women. They are lovers of mine. I don't want outsiders to speak to them. I must ask, because I could foresee some problematic situations arising.

This would be a permitted job, of course. Would your company be willing to sign confidentiality agreements? If so, I would love to set up a time for you to come here.

Regards,
Mark Black
Montecito, California

D_{ear} Mark,

As long as this will be a permitted job, I don't see a problem. We have worked on a number of projects that the company as well as each employee has had to sign a confidentiality agreement.

Andrew Hansen

Hansen Pool and Jacuzzis

$\mathcal{B}$

T o Minotti Furniture,

I am renovating my home this year, and one of the features in the extension is a great room for parties, which then leads to an indoor multiple pool area, which then leads to my version of a bordello, based on one I visited in Geneva when I was younger. The new space is approximately 24,000 square feet.

The arrangement of the space is mostly circular, because I studied the work of Le Corbusier when I was in college, and I always wanted to incorporate the non-linear approach to any residence I would one day be lucky enough to create. I have a friend who has taste, and he always tells me to purchase the furniture for the home at Minotti.

I was going to Pottery Barn for the rest of the house, but I now realize that people can tell the difference between antiques and replicas. So I gave all that furniture to charity and went to Paris, and I started filling my house with antiques. I must have bought a hundred pieces of furniture each day for two weeks. But I'm a modernist at heart, so for the extension I have designed it so that you feel like you're entering the new century, with a large barrier of aquariums and surreal aqua-screens that then lead to the addition. The transition is beautiful. But I need furniture!

Do you have the ability to furnish such a large space? My friend told me your space is small, so I wonder about it. There are other issues. I don't like couches and sofas, so I would like it to be all chairs. I also don't like end tables, but prefer low dining room tables to function as end tables without the use of dining room chairs. My parties can have as many as 1000 people, but of course they wouldn't all sit down at the same time. I have to host large events regularly. Usually about thirty percent would want seating at any given time. Would it be prohibitively costly to make 300–400 Arp or Capri chairs?

My friend tells me that is the design that would look best in there, if we were to order the right rugs. I am in Seoul on business right now, but am returning soon. I've had enough kimchee for two lifetimes. I would love to have a general idea about the possibilities your company can imagine, meanwhile.

Sincerely,

Mark Black

Montecito, California

Mark,

Thank you for your inquiry of Minotti furniture for your new project. Attached to this e-mail is a quote for both the Capri chair ($3,671.00 each) and the Arp chair ($3,271.00 each) in fabric. This is just so that you can get a general idea of what these pieces cost. In huge quantities such as the ones stated in the e-mail, the price will come down based on the final quantity. To answer your question about our ability to produce such high volume, Yes, Minotti has the capability to furnish a space such as yours. Our lead times are approximately 14–16 weeks, but based on the total quantity of product, it may have to be produced in phases. I am very interested in seeing the space. Is it possible to e-mail me a CAD file or a scale drawing? This will help me understand spatial relationships and the overall flow of the room. I will be glad to help you throughout this process of seeing your vision completed. I would like the opportunity to speak with you, so that we may discuss this in further detail.

Regards,

Christoff Alexis

Minotti Los Angeles

Dear Plessix Antiques,

I am decorating my large home with French antiques, but not really only furniture. I am more interested in artifacts that no one else has. The main objects I am looking for are antique wheelchairs and guillotines. It has a been lifelong dream of mine to own several of each.

Thank you,

Mark Black

Hello,
Thank you for visiting our Website, unfortunately we do not have anything like the items you described, we deal in 18th & 19th Century Antique furniture, artwork, and collectibles.
Plessix Antiques

Dear Ms. Curtis (Mythic Gardens),
I was staying at a Palm Springs hotel this year, and I admired how you approached the micro-experience of the garden atmosphere, so I requested your name from them, and they were responsive.

My main home is in a suburb of Konigsberg, Germany (remember Immanuel Kant?), and my dream would be to have you make it unique, but also with the characteristics, attributes, and qualities of that hotel I just mentioned above.

My wife and I built the small house next to a castle so that it looks like the castle is my house. It is a unique situation, because it creates a fantastic, almost aristocratic, effect.

My children are so happy we moved back here, because they didn't like living in Korea, where I had my business.

Now I have no garden, and it has been a sad summer. It is the opposite of my home in Mallorca, which had the gardens already coming with the house, which is two hundred years old. That would be wonderful to show you when you come to Europe. I have an interest in sharing those experiences with like-minded people.

My lover is a great cook, because her mother worked in the best restaurant in Seoul.

I'm in Mallorca for the next six weeks and don't have pictures with me. That was my error. My brother returns to the area next week, and I will ask him to take pictures.

It is a basic ranch house. The property is approximately one hectare. It is flat, but then the castle is just above it. I am curious to know your fee.

We are so happy in Germany now, basically, especially since the vacation to California.

Please share your thoughts about how you would like to proceed.
Sincerely,
Mark Black

Hello Mr. Black,

Many thanks for your kind e-mail and interest in my firm's work. I am on holiday with my family for the next two weeks, and I would happy to speak to you when I return. I hope you are enjoying your time in Mallorca, a colleague of mine is moving there this week. If you ever need any landscape lighting, you should let me know, and I will put you in touch with him. He does beautiful work and is a wonderful person.

Regarding your question about my fee, for projects involving travel, I bill on an hourly basis, with a cap that we are not to exceed. The cap is based on the project scope, and the minimum fee is $25,000 US and goes up from there, depending on scope, number of site visits, etc., plus reimbursement for meals, transportation, and accommodations. Please send the photos and any plans you have of the house and site when you have a moment. I look forward to hearing from you.

Best wishes,

Jenny Curtis, Mythic Gardens

Dear Schindler Elevators,

I would like to know about the possibility of installing escalators in my home. I have an elevator in one wing, but I'm not happy with it. I thought it would be a nice touch for my main addition to have escalators going to the two upper floors.

Do you have different models to consider?

Thank you,

Mark Black

Montecito, California

M_{ark,}

I have furnished and installed hundreds of residential elevators, but never an escalator. Most homes are not big enough.

I worked on Aaron Spelling's home, with 56,000 square feet, but all I installed was one 3,500 lb. commercial passenger elevator.

Best regards,

Robert Dale | New Construction Sales

Dear China Adoption Options,

I am thinking about adopting a child from your agency. We have a number of issues in our family unit, and I would like to make certain that we will be able to secure some kind of assurance that none of them will be a stumbling block when it comes to adoption.

I lived in Saudi Arabia before coming to the USA, and I arrived with four wives, although the government is only aware of one. The others are listed as friends. I already had a vasectomy, and three of my wives want children, so I plan to get nine children when I come to China. If that's a problem, maybe we can get nine children from nine different countries, spread out around the globe. Twins would be awesome, but does that mean sometimes there are triplets and quadruplets? They must be staggered in age so that it looks normal.

Our marriages are rather stable, although we are about to enter into therapy, mostly because my wives have become abusive with me, angry that I got a vasectomy. I believe some toddlers will distract them from me. We sometimes are shomer shabatt (we don't drive on Friday or Saturday, for example) and we pray five times a day as well. We follow a strict Kosher and Halal gluten-free, raw-food diet, and we participate in an international forum for nudists. Children are clothed at such events if they choose to be. We have members from China and Sweden.

I have enough space for all these people at my home, because I recently added a pavilion to my home here in California. I am in talks with a local installer about putting in an Olympic pool as well. I believe it will be a wonderful experience for the children we find. We are a very loving group!

I look forward to hearing from you about getting to the next step in our adoption journey.

Regards,

Mark Black

Montecito, California

Hi Mark,

We, nor any other agency, can issue guarantees for any international adoption programs. The eligibility requirements for each program are established by the foreign governments involved, and we have no control over those requirements.

Regarding how many children you can adopt from China—At this time, China only permits the adoption of 2 children at most, and that is only permissible if you adopt a Special Focus child through the Waiting Child Program (special needs children of all ages and healthy older children 8–13 years old). A Special Focus child is a child that has been in the Waiting Child Program for more than 2 months. If you are not open to adopting a Special Focus child, you would only be permitted to adopt one child at a time from China (unless it is twins, but that is extremely rare, and if China does not have any twins when it comes time for you to be matched with a child(ren), then you would be matched with a single child. If you refuse the referral simply because it is for a single child and not for twins, China will not give you another one.)

Regarding your family issues, your lifestyle and home life will be scrutinized by a social worker during the home-study phase of any adoption. You would not be able to adopt triplets or quadruplets from China. Other country programs do permit the adoption of sibling and non-related child groups. I would recommend reading the Outreach Guide I e-mailed to you yesterday to gain a better understanding of how the programs work and how many children you can adopt at one time.

For any home-study process, you are expected to provide full disclosure of your current family and life situation. You will also need to clear a background check with U.S. Citizenship and Immigration Services, as well as all adult members of your household. If you do not disclose something during your home study, it is possible that it will come up during the background check, and U.S. Citizenship and Immigration Services will deny your approval to immigrate a child into the U.S. All communications with any international adoption agency must be documented as well, to meet Hague requirements.

Please let me know if you have any questions, and thank you for your interest in adoption!

Sherry Taylor, International Adoption Consultant

CHAPTER TWELVE
MARK'S MARITAL NEEDS

Dear Marital Counselor,

I'm not sure how to approach marital counseling, given that I am involved in a marriage that is illegal. We need help, but require full confidentiality.

Although Jewish, I lived in Saudi Arabia for a number of years, where I adjusted my concept of marriage, eventually returning to this area with four wives. The federal government assumes that only one is actually my wife.

I am having major problems with three of my wives. The other one has been mine for only six months, and she is a total joy. Without her, I'd be less than nothing at this point. The rest have started ganging up on me, and I'm not sure how to handle it anymore. Recently they became physically abusive, taking advantage of the fact that I would never lay my hands on them. I believe it might be a custom for this sort of thing in the Gulf.

I've talked to other Jewish men who've married Saudi women (they were sane and married one), and they've reported similar issues to me. I can tell you more when I see you, but I am wondering how you would handle our sessions. Would you be giving me four independent sessions (one for each wife), or would you prefer meeting all at once?

Transportation isn't an issue if you choose either way, as I can hire a van to bring us. They all speak English and are totally civilized and educated. I think they read Gloria Steinem and some lesbian Marxist feminists while at school at Cambridge and I'm to suffer for all that men did to their maternal ancestors for centuries.

I am wondering if you've experience with polygamy, particularly regarding the intricacies of the sexual issues. Those are rather unique, as you can imagine. I had no idea when I got into this. Is it an interesting situation? Since it is my life, it seems so banal. Do you have experience with Saudi Arabians? Abuse of husbands by wives?

I look forward to hearing your suggestions.

Sincerely,

Mark Black

Hi Mark,

Very interesting situation to say the least, and YES all is confidential. My office is located in Beverly Hills. I would say it might be best to come separately with each one of them, and then if you wanted to do a session following that as a group, that is something we could pursue. You are also welcome to come by yourself for the first time, if you would like to explain the entire situation to me in greater detail. It is a unique situation, and I could imagine how complicated it must be, especially when it comes to the sexual issues.

I have worked with patients from some areas of the Middle East (Iran mostly), but not Saudi Arabia specifically. I have supervised missionaries and therapists who have worked with polygamy, but I have not worked with this in my caseload myself. And I have worked with husbands who have been abused, and of course, with women who have been abused as well.

If you want special expertise regarding Saudi Arabians, polygamy, and polygamy sexual relations, I would have to obtain outside consultation to be up to speed on those issues. I could also invite into our work a co-therapist with experience in those areas. Let me know if you have any further questions or would like to meet with me. Also let me know if you would like me to refer you to other therapists, instead.

One of the co-therapists is a woman who speaks both Hebrew and Arabic and has lived in Arab countries. I can find out whether she has expertise in polygamy and Saudi women in particular, if you would like.

Feel free to leave a phone number so we can chat, or you're welcome to try me at my office.

Warmly,

Dr. Mary Burke

Beverly Hills, California

Dear Spear Fishing Specialist,
I am coming to your area shortly and was wondering if shark spear fishing is particularly difficult. My marital counselor has suggested that a family adventure would do us a lot of good. I've always wanted to do this, but do you think it is something women would like? I have four wives (I once lived in Saudi Arabia) and nine adopted children. That means fourteen of us. Yes, an unusual bunch, but in some parts of the world it is the norm. We've had our share of marital malaise, but at this point we've made our peace. My wives are experienced fisherwoman, and my stepchildren learn quickly. I have a firm conviction that this outing will assist us with becoming far better both as individuals and as a family. The ocean heals everything, if you ask me. My stepchildren are all excellent swimmers, and my wives are too. One of them has gained so much weight I think she won't be able to go underwater (she floats!), but she'll do what she can. The pictures on your Website are really inspiring. You guys are heavy duty.
I look forward to hearing from you,
Mark Black

M<small>ark,</small>

Thanks for the inquiry. Sounds like you have your hands full!

I have traveled in the Middle East, so I am familiar with the family structures in some of the countries.

Spearfishing is a demanding sport that takes a lot of practice to get good at. You might be interested in a Great White Shark expedition instead. It is very easy, and you don't need to be scuba certified. We can arrange for a private charter for you and your family. Our charters are not cheap, though, and a week-long, live-aboard trip is about $5000.00 per person, so for 14 people it would be $70,000.00 approx. I am not sure if you planned to spend this kind of money or not? Let me know if you want to take this further.

Regards,

Mark Borelli

Dear Psychic,

My abilities and perceptions on all levels are failing me, and I understand that psychics don't have that problem. You guys are lucky you know whats. I've always been unlucky, except in business. But isn't that life, like my medieval philosophy professor used to remind us? I put it all together while we were having all-you-can-eat soft-shell crabs. Fatimah, a wife, has hired two private detective brothers, so I need to do one step better and get help from a parapsychological detective. She is suspicious that I've hidden a ton of money from her. Chest pains are starting to plague me, and I'm worried about my future, because no matter what I do, I am tormented by the women I've chosen to live with. Luxury living on my estate doesn't seem to be enough, as well as the live-in masseuses, the trips to St. Tropez, Bali and so forth. You'd think it would be. You'd think I would get some *shukran* (thank you, in Arabic) for all that I have given. I have talked to my rabbi ("have them convert") and my marital therapist ("y'all have to communicate better") about how I feel abused, but I no longer know if their advice is helping. Despair is what I think we can call this. It is a blackish hole of confusion. I want to know that my nine adopted children will be cared for. That's why I returned here from Saudi Arabia. But my hope has dried up. I see nothing. I see an end. I need your help to tell me if this is true. I can make peace with it, if that is the case. I can let go and allow myself to fade. Fatimah is a mystic, and she tells me you can do this for me, that's why you're in this profession. The same expertise and discipline that I've brought to my luxury consultancy business as I've crafted my career is what I'm told you apply. Please tell me what's going to happen, even if it just means this month/year, but preferably two years.

Yours sincerely,

Mark Black

Montecito, California

Dear Mark,

I am not sure I can help you. I am an astrologer, a psychic, and a medium. You are involved in a very messy situation which needs cleaning up, and I'm not sure you are open to doing that. If I do anything for you, you will need to fly yourself and your wives here to where I work (Tucson). When I do readings, I do not mince words. I tell it like it is. There is a great deal of dark energy around you, because of the situation you're in. You need negative-energy clearing as well as guidance to let go of some of your situation. That's all I will say at this time.

Sally Johnson

Then, ten minutes later:

M ark,
My Spirit team just came in and told me I cannot help you with your
situation, so you are going to have to find someone else, so please do
that and don't contact me again. You are loaded with negative entities
and other stuff I don't wish to deal with. Thank you for respecting my
wishes.
Sally Johnson

Dear Astrologer,

I am contacting you near the end of my journey, after having been through a tremendous amount of agony and pleasure satisfying my many needs, even though I couldn't get a birthday reservation at the French Laundry, but I have satisfied many of mine, as well as those of my wives. It all feels so unreal, but it is so painful I can't pretend it is.

It is of upmost importance that we keep this confidential, because my wives seem to have hired two Chinese private investigators that are monitoring my movements and psychological states both here and from Shanghai, where I am moving one of my business headquarters, ever since we had a rough afternoon with a psychotherapist in Beverly Hills, as well as a polygamy specialist she'd brought in who was a sub-specialist in Saudi women and spousal abuse by wives. The one condition set by Fatimah, the mystical one of the four wives, for not having a general strike at my property here in Montecito and losing all my wives, is that we appeal to the help of an astrologer to solve our problems. Therapy has its limits, and my cardiologist thinks I can't sustain any more of this marital stress, saying I can't resolve everything by purchasing these women super-cars and adding more chairs to our unique home design. I wish you'd seen the parties I'd thrown for Fatimah (the open barrels of Beluga caviar), and she's ungrateful. But I spent twenty-two years flying back and forth between Germany and Saudi Arabia trying to get her, having played the cello for her and written devotional poetry to her being, which her authoritarian father resented me for until the day he passed away peacefully, just as I was flying back into town. Fatimah is the moodiest person you've ever encountered. I can't keep enough crystal in the house. She smashes it, but as extreme as her volatility is, you can't imagine how wonderful she is when she is joyful. She makes me feel like I did when I still believed the only thing there was in the universe was my mother.

That's where you come in. My mother (Shoshana) was born on June 29, and Fatimah was born on June 18, and I was born on December 21. Majida, wife #2 (again, the government only knows about one wife), is June 7. Aisha, #3, is June 11. The latest wife, of six months, also named Fatima (without the H at the end), is August 25. I'm particularly interested in the possible compatibilities of these dates, as well as how you predict the coming two years will be for us. I believe that, as these women transition into converting to Judaism while following my raw-food diet, it will be stressful on all of us, plus there's construction of an Olympic pool that is taking forever.

I'm open to all your suggestions regarding how you think I can manage this from an astrological perspective. Fatimah might be able to relax once I can prove to her that the stars aren't against us, as she has suggested, especially this month. She's ruined at least ten dinners and a handful of beautiful afternoon strolls.

If you consider it important to come meet us I can make arrangements for it, but in that case I would need to know how you feel you could be helpful, because I would need to present the case for you to visit to Majida, as she is an attorney and is now deeply private and paranoid, knowing that polygamy is illegal in this country, and she fears imprisonment or deportation.

Sorting all this out sooner than later astrologically so that I don't have to go back to the therapist's for another six hour session (one private hour, one hour with each wife, and one group hour) would be enormously helpful.

Yours sincerely,

Mark Black

Montecito, California

Dear Mark,

I'm glad you shared with me, and I understand, and I am sorry for all that you are going thru, because you worked hard all your life, and now when you can enjoy it all, you have this happen to you.

I would strongly recommend some clearing work for you and the wife who has the extreme mood swings in particular. Also has she been evaluated for bipolarity or manic depression? I'm wondering if some mood stabilizer may be helpful for her.

I am more than happy to meet with you or talk on the phone. I would analyze your chart and the impact of each of your wives' charts to each other and to you, as well as the transits and how the planetary conditions are impacting each of you and the whole group dynamic. I also specialize in soul-level connections and use the 9th harmonic chart, or chart of the soul mate, which can shed a lot of light on these matters and incorporate some of the Magi Astrology techniques, which look at Nuclear Blasts, Saturn Clashes, Captivization, Golden Linkages, Soul Mates and other dynamics that can provide great insight into relationship and group dynamics.

The psychic work I do will allow me to access the karmic and past-life dimensions to the situation and provide some spiritual guidance on how to proceed, as well as the different paths that may be taken at this time as well as counseling as appropriate. Please feel free to write, or we can set up some time on the phone where I can describe a bit more about how I work.

What is nice, you are understanding the situation very well, and have reached out for help. I had a similar situation happen a Dr. in Bel Air, and the person he loved, and was able to help him, and now he is doing very well, and things are back to normal with him. He left Bel Air, and is now living quietly with his wife and six children in Hawaii.

I look forward to working with you. You take care, and I will keep you in my prayers!

Best Regards,

Annie Hansford

CHAPTER THIRTEEN
MARK'S LETTER TO THE PRESIDENT

The White House
1600 Pennsylvania Avenue NW
Washington, DC 20500

Dear President Barack Obama,

First of all, I offer my congratulations to you. Second, to myself, because I am finally home (as a side note, you have no idea what a hellhole Saudi Arabia is) to the great country you now administer. What a burden that must be, *Oy Gevalt.*

All I have to deal with are a couple acres south of Santa Barbara, plus a number of zany people that I've foolishly invited to be with me. I have everything now, all that the world can offer, and some headaches. A house with an escalator (I don't think yours has that) and a glass pavilion, plus more love from those that love me than I can really handle. Imagine that for a moment, being smothered, as if in a harem.

It is my turn to celebrate after so many of years of sorrow and ennui, due mostly to my silly undertaking of reading the whole of the philosophical and literary canon. How many people do you know who reread Beowulf and Trollope?

Now, as for you, please ignore those that offer ignorant opinions on things. If there's anything I've learned, and I've written to thousands of people, it is that all you have to do is ask the right person to get the right answer.

The question contains the answer, in other words.

In other words, we already know what they're going to say.

Better stated, clarification of reality can only occur within our souls, before reality (which doesn't really exist) has a chance to pollute you.

A consequence of my discovery that there is no reality is that I know nothing. I am conservative by nature, both politically and fiscally. Augustine wrote his confessions to a woman at a brothel, I believe, and I am telling you my woes instead of the UCSB student bartender at Lucky's, an overpriced place down the street, lined with super-cars. Why? Because you are the First Man in the world, and there is a chance that you'll deserve it, but I guess it remains to be seen, since the proof is in the pudding.

Unlike you, I am a miserable public speaker. Like you, I love to communicate. I'd be depressed if I had to address the world. Unlike most people, I might admit to being an elitist. Like most people of my rank and stature, I pretend I want a democracy. Something authentic and representative, I guess.

Really, if you really want to know, I wish I were royalty, since that would have saved me a lot of lousy mornings waking up to an alarm clock that I wanted to throw out of my top floor condominiums in Riyadh and Riga, where I used to have to live part-time, thanks to a small woman named Fatimah and a physical therapist named Velna. That concerns a book I hope one day to publish and win the Nobel with. It is called *One Hundred Thousand Nights of Agony as I Flew to Saudi Arabia in Search of Her.* I hope you like the title because I like the titles of yours.

If you have any words of encouragement or solace you feel you can offer me as I deal with all the issues in my life, I would be grateful. Let's face it, I'm an erudite mess.

I wish I had known you on your way up. I almost got close to George W. Now it is next to impossible. But if you think of it, in your next State of the Union Address, use your left eye to give me a wink. That would make my life closer to something like the perfection I am after. It already is sort of okay the way it is, but it would seal the experience.

Your fellow citizen of the world,

Mark Black

THE END